there is no backstage

"Linda Stephens is one of the finest actors of her generation. In her insightful and moving reflections on 50 years in the professional theatre, Linda shares her journey through almost every possible venue for theatre. From auspicious beginnings in dinner theatre, to regional theatre to Broadway, she has created a successful and fulfilling career. In this sensitive and beautifully written memoir, Linda reveals the struggles, triumphs, dedication, and above all, the ultimate grace found in a life in the theatre. Every actor would benefit from reading this brilliant and enlightening tribute to the working craftspeople and supreme artists of the acting profession."

David H. Bell
Head of the Music Theatre Program at Northwestern University
Former Artistic director of Ford's Theatre, Associate Artistic Director
of The Alliance Theatre. Multi-award-winning writer/director of the
JOSEPH JEFFERSON in Chicago, THE HELEN HAYES in DC,
and THE OLIVIER Nominee for HOT MIKADO in London

"The title of this rich and entertaining memoir has a very specific meaning as spoken to the author by a colleague and reported in the book. The book being an account of the author's life both onstage and off, the title broadens to suggest that the two realms aren't as different as is often thought. Both require clarity and courage and belief. As did the composition of this absorbing story of a life in art."

Amlin Gray
Playwright
OBIE Award winner for HOW I GOT THAT STORY,
GUGGENHEIM Fellow for Creative Arts US and Canada

"This is one of the best books I've ever read about the life of an actor, not a celebrity mind you, but a prodigiously talented working actor. It is an honest, unflinching, generous, and warm-spirited look at what it means to dedicate your life to a profession that demands so much and can give back so little. As Linda so beautifully chronicles however, when it does give back, it can change lives forever. Every young actor at the start of their career should read this book to better understand the capricious and heartbreaking, yet often rewarding and shimmering life that may await them."

Don Spalding
Director, Patron Program, CARNEGIE HALL

"Linda Stephens tells us early on in this poignant, life-affirming memoir that one knows one has become an actor when the need to express the work becomes more important than the desire to express oneself. Lucky us, that she willingly shares so much about her own incredible life, taking us on a journey from small-town Arkansas to Broadway, while imparting hard-earned life's lessons involving relationships, work-life balance, aging, and, most of all, the highs and lows of a working actor's life. True to her title, there's no backstage in this remarkably honest, vulnerable and wise account of a full life lived on the world's stage."

Mike Fischer
Wisconsin Theatre Dramaturg
Member of Forward Theater Artist Collective in Madison,
Nine years CHIEF DRAMA CRITIC for the Milwaukee Journal Sentinel

"*There is No Backstage* is distinguished actor Linda Stephens' remarkable memoir of five decades in the theater and her debut as an engaging story-teller. Her voice brings you right to the front row and evokes *Time Magazine's* review of her in the 1994 Broadway revival of DAMN YANKEES: "Linda Stephens makes a stunning Broadway debut!" She takes us on a journey of openness, humility and depth into her award-winning career until the book's poignant finale. She weaves a narrative of family, love, and nuanced details of a professional actor's life work, the many dimensions impossible for an audience to know. What a privilege to be invited in. *Backstage* brought me to my feet in a standing ovation. Bravo!"

Louisa Loveridge-Gallas
Poet and Writer
Revelations on Longing Street, Earth Solutions Press;
Rescue The Good Stuff, Zaragueya Press; Wizard's Dream,
ERIC HOFFER FOUNDATION AWARD: Singing Road Press

Book Designed by Michael Proft

Unless otherwise credited, all photographs are courtesy of the author

The Library of Congress has catalogued this book as follows:

Stephens, Linda W

THERE IS NO BACKSTAGE: An Actor's Life/A Memoir by Linda Stephens
p. cm.
ISBN 978-1-7923-8782-1
TXu 2-309-276   2022

This book was set in Sabon.

there is no backstage

an actor's life

A MEMOIR

LINDA STEPHENS

To The Working Actor

"It has been said that an actor must have the hide of a rhinoceros, the courage and audacity of a lion, and most importantly, the fragile vulnerability of an egg. It also has been said that the moment of not knowing is the moment that has the greatest potential for creativity. The professional and private lives of most actors are filled to the brim with moments of not knowing.

Actors are survivors and will continue to strive because they have the need to celebrate, in performance, that sacred communion between actor and audience."

Robert Prosky
Film and Arena Stage Company Actor
1930—2008

ACKNOWLEDGMENTS

To my writer friends who've given their time to read and respond to this fledgling memoir, thanks to Eleanor Ringel, Amlin Gray, Jeff Lunden, David Bell, Mike Fischer, Paul Salsini and Steve Warren. Special thanks go to Jennifer Rupp for her early encouragement, to Lee Smith for her knowing and kind guidance, to Susan Loveridge for always being there, to Mari McCarty for her loving support, and to Louisa Loveridge-Gallas for her generosity and ongoing belief in my work.

To my friends who've given personal feedback, many thanks to Rosemary Prinz, Don Spalding, Terry Beaver, Pat Crump, Sandra Deer, Brenda Bynum, Jim Loveridge, Julie Swenson, Jennifer Uphoff-Gray, Pam Kriger, Alex Rybeck and Gwen Benner.

To my sister and brother-in-law, Lorna and Mark, thank you for your love and approval. I love you more than I know how to say.

A huge thank you goes to Michael Proft for being not only primary hand-holder and witness to my book as it unfolded through the pandemic years of 2020/21/22, but for his beautiful book design. I could not have completed this book without Michael's ear and artistry.

And finally, I give thanks to my ex-husband Kent Stephens for giving me permission to write about our professional and personal lives together. His only request was that I exercise forgiveness and be kind. I believe I've honored his request.

INTRODUCTION

You may not know who I am. Yet, I've been acting on stages for fifty years. I've played one hundred fifty roles in at least five thousand performances. I've worked with hundreds of actors, directors, musicians, designers and technicians. I've worked with icons of the theatre—Tennessee Williams, Arthur Miller, Stephen Sondheim.

You won't know who I am unless you saw me on Broadway or in Chicago at Steppenwolf and The Goodman in the '90's, or at the Alliance Theatre in Atlanta in the '80's, or The Harlequin in Washington, DC in the 70's, or on the stages of a dozen or more regional theatres across the country. I've been given Best Actress Awards for my work in New York, Chicago, Atlanta, Miami and Washington, DC. Yet, you may not know who I am.

I can hardly believe my life in the theatre. I didn't set out to be an actor. I was not trained as an actor. But acting is the work that was given, so I have to believe that acting is the work I was supposed to do. But how is it that I became an actor? How is it that my life's work has been about pretending to be other people, interpreting other peoples' words?

The great acting teacher Sanford Meisner said that it takes twenty years to become an actor. I passed that milestone more than thirty years ago. But how it happened that acting became my profession and remained so these fifty years is a kind of mystery to me.

This memoir is an exploration of that mystery. It's a meander through the passages of my experience in search of understanding all that has gone into the making of this actor's life.

CHAPTER ONE

beginnings

*"I could've spread my wings and done a thousand things
I've never done before."*

Eliza Doolittle, MY FAIR LADY

My mother told me that when I was four years old, I walked into a room full of adults sitting around after dinner, sang "Silent Night" from beginning to end and silenced the room. It seems that I declared myself a singer very early on.

But the actress in me wasn't born until the spring of 1968, in a first-time collaboration between the music and drama schools at Illinois Wesleyan University, in a production of MY FAIR LADY. From the music school I was cast as Eliza Doolittle. From the drama school Larry Shue was cast as Henry Higgins.

Larry Shue—beloved Larry Shue, brilliant Larry Shue—who would become known as the playwright of THE NERD, THE FOREIGNER, GRANDMA DUCK IS DEAD, AND WENCESLAS SQUARE. Larry Shue, who at age thirty-nine would pass away, when the small plane he was traveling on from Richmond to Staunton, Virginia, flew into the side of a mountain overlooking the Shenandoah Valley. It was 1985.

But in 1968, during our run of MY FAIR LADY, every night I was challenged to rise to Larry's dazzling performance, and every night before the bows, he would take me in his arms in the dark backstage and give me a whopper of a kiss. My opening night present from him was not a bunch of roses, but a live guinea pig he named "Eliza." I fell head over heels for Larry Shue and his shock of roan-colored hair, and his wickedly smart sense of humor. What else could I do? I had no choice but to fall in love. So, our show crush became an engagement and the following September became a marriage. Neither of us had lived anywhere but our parents' houses and college dorms. According to Larry, all the other graduating actors were going to New York, so we should take the Southwest Chief from Chicago to Hollywood. And that's what we did. Larry was twenty-two. I was twenty-one.

We arrived in Los Angeles in the fall of 1969. The first military draft numbers were chosen December first of 1969. When they were chosen, Larry's number was one hundred seventy-two of the three hundred sixty-six numbers chosen, which meant he would likely be called to serve sooner rather than later. The Vietnam war was at its angry height, so the thought of being drafted into the army was very scary. There was nothing to do except wait for the army to call. In the meantime, Larry found work in LA almost immediately, acting in a new play in a small theatre company. And he was an extra in several films, including a Beau Bridges film called GAILY, GAILY. I also found work and joined my first union, AGMA—American Guild of Musical Artists—the union for opera and dance, so that I might sing with the Euterpe Opera Club. Their productions were performed in the late mornings at the Dorothy Chandler Pavilion where the Academy Awards were held at the time.

My first and only opera with Euterpe was a new work about Joan of Arc. I was the soprano of three female choristers who narrated the story. I remember one lyric, "While victory lags, the king must wear rags, so out goes the tailor, he hasn't a chance of stitching for France." I don't remember anyone's name, but I remember that bizarre lyric and the melody that went with it. Funny how melody activates memory. I would learn more about melody's effect on memory when eleven years from then I would play my most important role, a stroke victim named Emily Stilson in a production of Arthur Kopit's WINGS.

But in 1969, alongside singing opera in the mornings, I did temp work in LA. One day I was called to be a receptionist at Paramount Studios in the office of a Mr. Smith. I arrived early before anyone was in the office. I took my place behind the front desk, answered a few calls and took messages, until an hour later a man named Allan Carr walked in and said "Good Morning." He asked me what I did, and I told him I was an actress. "What's your name?" he said. "Linda Shue." I said. "Sounds like a sneeze," he said. "You should change that." Then he went into his office.

Another hour passed before Mr. Smith walked in, a gorgeous man with a perfect California tan. I nearly fell off my chair when he introduced himself with "Call me Roger." Mr. Roger Smith. 77 *Sunset Strip* Roger Smith. Ann-Margret's husband Roger Smith. And now he was working alongside award-winning producer Allan Carr, in their newly created Rogallan Productions.

One day they invited me to lunch with William Holden. Yes, *the* William Holden. He was wearing Roger's same California tan. It was surreal. When Mr. Holden asked if I'd like lemon or milk with my tea, I said "Both," and the milk curdled. Of course. I wasn't thinking. They were kind. They said nothing. How naïve I was.

A couple of weeks later when the job with Rogallan was over, I was called by the temp agency to see if I played piano well enough to be accompanist for a voice teacher. I didn't, but I said yes anyway. Turns out the teacher was the singing coach for The Smothers Brothers Show, so I was accompanist for the show's dancers. Amazing. I would refuse the job now. But then I was fearless, or naïve, or fearless because I was naïve. And I was very good at faking it. Maybe that's how we all start in life, by faking until we realize we're faking, and then we lose our chutzpah.

The singing coach kept me on for a few months more, before finding a better accompanist. Kind of her.

The government finally called for Larry in LA, so he flew to San Francisco for a week to establish residency there, hoping to delay entry into the army for a few months more. We'd been cast in a season of summer stock for a new company in Oshkosh, Wisconsin, and Larry wanted to make sure we honored our commitment.

Gary Bruch was a fellow Wesleyan classmate who'd rented the old Orpheum circuit-era Grand Opera House in Oshkosh, WI. We'd perform there in the premiere season of The Eldon Bruch Repertory Theatre Company, named for Gary's father. But during early rehearsals, the government caught up with Larry again. He was to be drafted into the army within a couple of weeks. Larry requested a deferred entry, so that we could honor our summer contract. But the deferral meant that he would serve three instead of two years in the army. It's what he did for love.

That summer Larry played Sir in THE ROAR OF THE GREASEPAINT, THE SMELL OF THE CROWD, The Emperor in his own children's musical MY EMPEROR'S NEW CLOTHES, Felix in THE ODD COUPLE, Dracula in DRACULA, and my father in THE FANTASTICKS.

I played Luisa in THE FANTASTICKS, The Woman in THE ROAR

OF THE GREASEPAINT, THE SMELL OF THE CROWD, and I played the piano in the pit for MY EMPEROR'S NEW CLOTHES. I also ran the bat for DRACULA.

I'd cracked the fifth metatarsal of my right foot, tripping down the stairs in our actor housing, just a week before DRACULA went into rehearsal. So, instead of being in the show, I stood backstage on crutches holding one end of a rope, on the other end of which was attached the paper maché bat hovering just offstage. When it was time for the bat's entrance, I'd lean forward as far as my crutches would allow, let the rope slide through my hands to send the bat swooping onto the stage. Then when the bat had done its job, I'd quickly pull the creature offstage, and ground my crutches again. These were the days before digitalization and sometimes mechanization. In this case I supplied the mechanics.

I also worked the trap door that allowed Larry/Dracula to disappear. I'd stand in the very small trap room under the stage, crutches and all, and release the smoke from the dry ice canister until it filled the room. I'd wait, taking shallow breaths until it was time for Dracula to disappear from stage. Then I'd pull the rope that opened the trap door as the smoke ascended to stage and Larry descended. We'd stand belly to belly in the small room till the trap door closed, then we'd rush to the hallway where we could breathe fresh air—as fresh as air could be in the basement of an opera house built in 1883. It was a dangerous thing to have done. We both had scrapes from the ropes and the tiny trap door. But we were naïve, and fearless because we were naïve, and at that point in our actor lives, the show was all. It's what we did for love.

There was a time that summer when the company ran out of money and there was talk of closing before the end of our short season. One evening I was onstage with Larry, painting flats for the next night's opening. We were listening to an argument coming from the back of the house between Gary and his father, who was the sole producer for the season. His father was also naïve. There hadn't been enough advertising. There had been no presales. The belief was that "If you build it, they will come." But of course, they don't. Theatre isn't that easy. This wouldn't be my last experience going through the death of a theatre because of too-high expectations at the box office. But now, as there was only one more play to do, Gary's father decided to bite the bullet, foot the bill, and chalk it up as loss and a lesson hard-learned. Kind of him.

That summer before Larry went into basic training for the army, was a kind of basic training in theatre for me. We were interns not only to acting. We were interns to the theatre of our own making. We did everything. We built the sets. We hawked the shows on the streets. We cleaned the bathrooms. We played the lead in one show and ran the bat in the next. We were the runners as well as the stars. And we held our salaries when the box office sales were small. That summer planted the seed of my life as a working actor.

Only a few days after our final performance, Larry was drafted. He was called for ten weeks basic training in Texas. Then after an additional three weeks of specialist training, he was stationed at Fort Lee in Petersburg, Virginia. I'd gone to live with my family during his time away, until I could join him in Virginia, where I lived in a Petersburg hotel while Larry was still in the barracks. We looked for suitable off-base housing for both of us, and found a park of converted trailers for rent, about twenty miles from base. We lived there for a few months until we found a home closer to Fort Lee. It was an upstairs apartment in an old duplex in downtown Petersburg, across the street from the Brown and Williamson tobacco factory. The sweet, almost acrid smell of roasting tobacco lived with us 24-7, but we were happy because we were together. And we were doing theatre—army theatre.

Larry had landed in the Army's Special Services. Larry was a visual artist as well as an actor, so the Army decided that the best way Larry could serve, was by drawing caricatures for posters of the plays he would also perform in. He had a desk job during the day, but at night he did theatre. Fort Lee had and still has a theatre company, so Larry and I became central to helping mount and perform in plays. We did Murray Schisgal's LUV, THE WALTZ OF THE TOREADORS, and WEST SIDE STORY. I was Maria, and Larry one of the Jets. I even put together a cabaret for the officers, and was awarded the "Certificate of Community Achievement" signed by Major General John D. McLaughlin, then Commanding General. Larry would tell people that he wasn't the only one in the army, that we both were.

Our first audience for WEST SIDE STORY was nine hundred soldiers in basic training, marched into the theatre by their officers. Seeing our show was mandatory. All night long there were whistles and shouts and cat calls from the boys, especially when we actresses were onstage. I was humiliated and very angry at the crowd—so angry that I refused to take my curtain call. Larry was upset with me. He told me that my responsibility was to the audience, no matter how they reacted. He told me we were lucky that they wanted to respond at all, that basic training had been close to hell on earth for him and these guys were going through that same hell. I was still angry, but I heard Larry. He was telling me to focus on the work, not myself.

A few years ago, I taught a masterclass for musical theatre students. I gave them the Sanford Meisner quote about it taking twenty years to become an actor. One of the students asked, "How do you know when you've become an actor?" I've thought about that over the years, and I'm not sure what I told him then, but what I say now is that you know you've become an actor when your need to express the work has become more important than your need to express yourself. Stanislavski says it this way, "Love the art in yourself, not yourself in the art."

What is that art in ourselves? What is acting? Besides declaring that it takes twenty years to become an actor, Sanford Meisner also said: "Acting is behaving truthfully within imaginary circumstances." And, according to Shakespeare in his advice to the players in HAMLET, acting is "holding as 'twere, a mirror up to nature." And because that mirror is charged with reflecting the truth of human nature, I believe that acting can be healing, not only for the audience but also for the holder of the mirror.

While Larry was still in the army, we not only did army theatre, we also did dinner theatre at Swift Creek Mill Playhouse in Colonial Heights, Virginia. PLAY IT AGAIN SAM, THE DECLINE AND FALL OF THE ENTIRE WORLD AS SEEN THROUGH THE EYES OF COLE PORTER, FIDDLER ON THE ROOF, 1776. During the days, Larry would do his army secretarial work. It's amazing to think of now. How theatre-rich that time was. But there was a point when Larry was on orders for Vietnam. I didn't know. He didn't tell me. Larry had been horrified to learn that all the men he'd done basic training with had been sent to Vietnam. No young man belonged in Vietnam. Larry certainly did not belong in Vietnam. One of his senior officers knew that, and got Larry's orders dismissed. It was a blessing.

Three years later, when Larry's service at Fort Lee was finished, we moved to Washington, DC. A year before we'd made a trip to

Arena Stage, the large regional theatre in DC, and had met with a young man who'd told us that we could be interns for the next year's season at Arena. Turns out that the young man was an intern himself and was now long gone. We hadn't understood that his promise had been only a possibility. So, here we were committed to a year's lease on an apartment in Alexandria, Virginia, with no work and no idea what we were going to do. We were so naïve.

But Larry saw everything as an adventure. He was the most joyful person I've ever known. I asked him once, when he walked down a familiar street, did it look the same to him as it had the day before. And he said "Oh, no, it's different every day! Everything is new all the time!" Well. I'm still learning to see the world the way he did. Ours was an attraction of opposites. I tended toward melancholy. And Larry, joy. He used to call us Thalia and Melpomene—Comedy and Tragedy. And that we were. I think it's fair to say that Larry was my first acting coach. Sharing stage with him was a lesson in character-building, storytelling, playing an audience and loving them.

It may also be that Larry was my first life coach. In 2016, when I was sixty-nine, I played Betty Meeks, the old gal in Larry's play, THE FOREIGNER at the Milwaukee Rep, the theatre where the play had premiered in 1983. It was a beautiful reminder of the joy of Larry Shue, of his never-ending love of life which was still shining through his storytelling over thirty years after his death. His biggest lesson for me? Love your audience. Like all actors, Larry wanted to be loved by the audience. But more important, he loved his audience. He loved people. He studied people. And when he died there were memorials all over the country where people, artists and audience alike, thought Larry was their best friend. He was. He was best friend to all of them. Larry belonged to us all.

We did find work in DC sooner than we imagined we would. Only months after our move, we auditioned for the first production of the newly formed Harlequin Dinner Theatre in Rockville, Maryland. The show was PROMISES, PROMISES. We were both cast. It was to be the first of many musicals we'd do both there and in Atlanta, where we'd build a second theatre a few years down the road. Larry and I would become two of a company of players that would do some of the best musical theatre in that or any other city. It was our coming-of-age theatre. It was a coming together of artists so fertile, that to this day, fifty years later, people still remember the acting company of The Harlequin.

CHAPTER TWO

atlanta

"Simple little things. Simple little dreams will do."

Lizzie Curry, 110 IN THE SHADE

The interior of the newly built Harlequin-Atlanta was a beautiful rough-hewn wooden space with upper and lower levels reminiscent of Shakespeare's Globe. But in place of standing room for the groundlings, there were tables for pre-show diners with lanterns that gave off a golden glow.

We'd opened the theatre with WHERE'S CHARLEY? which was a great success. Our second production was 110 IN THE SHADE, the musical version of THE RAINMAKER by Harvey Schmidt and Tom Jones. I would be privileged to work with Tom and Harvey ten years from then in their musical version of OUR TOWN called GROVERS CORNERS. But in 1975 at The Harlequin, opening night of their 110 IN THE SHADE was a night we would never forget.

The story is about a huckster called Starbuck who comes to a small drought-ridden Texas town and fools everyone into believing he can make rain, except for Lizzie Curry. I was playing the plain-speaking Lizzie, who knows he's bluffing and challenges him, till he convinces her to open her heart to the possibility of all things. And when she does, the rains miraculously come.

During tech week for our production, the rains wouldn't come. The Harlequin-Atlanta's stage was wide and high. Our techies had tried everything they could to create enough pressure for the water coming from ground-level to reach the pipes atop the high proscenium, so that when the valves were opened, water could shower down onto the stage. But they hadn't found a way to make it work. So, we went into opening night expecting the most important character in the play to be absent. The audience would have to imagine the rain.

But the techies never stopped tinkering. They didn't believe their final adjustments could possibly work, till the last scene of the play when the thunder rolled, and the rains came! A cheer rose from the balcony where our producers and staff were on their feet. Applause from the audience below came along with waves of laughter that nearly drowned out the orchestra. It was a glorious moment standing onstage among a chorus of actors being dowsed with water falling from "the sky," all of us singing "Cumulo Nimbo!" The miracle of the story had become the miracle of our production. Belief in possibility.

While the rain pelted our cast onstage, I stood in the wings waiting to take my bow and watched. Our Starbuck, Jack Kyrieleison, entered stage for his bow, ripped off his cowboy hat and flung the rain onto the audience. Lord have mercy! With the flourish of his hat, Jack expressed joy for all of us in this amazing opening night in the theatre we'd built, we band of Harlequin players. It was wonderful!

Larry and I along with Jack and Michele Mundell, the two of whom would one day marry, were the "core" of our company of players. Years later, when I was working at The Kennedy Center, Michele came to see my show. After the matinee, I met her at the stage door where the security guard had just let her through the gate. He looked at the two of us and asked, "Are you sisters?" Michele and I took a beat, looked at one another, and happily said, "Yes!" Michele, Jack and I have a lifelong bond.

The Harlequin gave me so much. Above all it taught me the value of working within a company. We made theatre together. And like that summer of stock in Oshkosh, Wisconsin, we did everything. We made costumes. We built sets. We waited tables. We played in the orchestra. We rehearsed in the day, and we performed at night. We acted together. We drank together. We even lived together in Rockville in the converted cabins of an old motel a few miles from the theatre, where on Mondays off we'd drag chairs to the center circle of lawn surrounded by the rebuilt cabins, and drink gin and tonics in the late summer afternoons. And through all of this we were honing our craft in the doing of our craft. We were a non-union company, but we were pros from the beginning. What is a pro? Someone who does the work for a living. And theatre was our living in all ways. We were paid for our work, but more important, we lived our work.

Our kind of company doesn't exist any longer. It can't really in our corporate world where decisions are made from the top down without significant input from those doing the hands-on work. In the past as with The Harlequin, many regional theatres had resident acting companies, and the acting company was still a part of the theatre's creative process. Now nearly all resident acting companies established for decades have been dissolved. And with that dissolution, these company actors have been sent out into the "market," often for the first time, mid-career, to find work from show to show. Their job having become as much about getting the work as doing the work.

I believe also that the quality of the work has changed. To lift a statement from Alan Arkin's autobiography—there are two kinds of actor, those who want to create effect, and those who want to create experience. It seems to me that there are now more actors in the world whose primary goal is to create effect. And I believe part of the reason is that more energy is spent in selling oneself to get the job, than in doing the work.

Bob Prosky, one of the original company members of Arena Stage in Washington, DC once said, "I love performance. That time when the human beings onstage interact with the human beings in the audience, and together they create the event of performance." Together they've created more than effect. They've created experience.

I played fifteen roles at The Harlequin from 1972 to 1976 and among them were Guinevere in CAMELOT, Abigail Adams in 1776, Rosemary in HOW TO SUCCEED IN BUSINESS WITHOUT REALLY TRYING, and Lizzie Curry, the first of my signature roles in 110 IN THE SHADE. The Harlequin would be the second theatre company I'd watch fail based on too-high an expectation at the box office. But even in The Harlequin's demise it gave me more.

It gave me home. For a time. I was to stop moving and put down roots in Atlanta. And like the city that's continued to "burn to the ground" and rebuild itself since Sherman marched through town on his way to the sea, I rebuilt myself in Atlanta. The Harlequin had introduced my work to Fred Chappell, artistic director of The Alliance Theatre, the large regional theatre in the Atlanta. Edith Love, then managing director, would eventually call me the "leading lady of choice" in the 1980's. I was to move from musical to straight theatre. And I was to move from one marriage to a second, from Larry Shue to Kent Stephens—intensely gifted Kent Stephens—singer, writer, actor, director, and artistic director of his own alternative theatre. The Imaginary Theatre.

the imaginary theatre

"Something under way here ... light is getting brighter ..."

Emily Stilson, WINGS

Kent Stephens opened my mind to a kind of theatre I'd never known. He taught me to explore my characters more deeply, to understand more completely the words I spoke. He taught me the difference between repeating and recreating a performance from night to night. He helped me become a better actor. We met playing opposite one another on the Harlequin stage doing Shakespeare in the mornings for high school audiences. I was playing Olivia and he was Sebastian in TWELFTH NIGHT. Larry was playing Malvolio. Larry was also playing Tevye on the same stage in the evenings in our production of FIDDLER ON THE ROOF, and I was playing his oldest daughter Tzeitel. For three weeks every night my Tzeitel would weep at Larry/Tevye's feet pleading for him to allow her to marry the man she loved, and every morning my Olivia would fall in love with Kent/Sebastian. My life was unreal. I was living a romantic fantasy, and I couldn't tell the difference between what I was feeling, and what was true.

The Harlequin was struggling. And like that summer of stock in

Oshkosh, we all were holding our salaries in the hope that audiences would grow and that the theatre would begin to break even. Larry and I were holding our hearts separate from one another. I was pouring mine into the romance of the stories we were telling, and Larry was pouring his into doing what he did best, into making his audience happy. Our marriage had become a mirror of the theatre's struggle, and so along with The Harlequin I let our marriage go. And yes, within the year I married another show crush. Still naïve. Kent was twenty-four, and I was thirty.

Like Larry and I, Kent and I made theatre together. I worked with Kent in his newly-created Imaginary Theatre. Kent made a kind of theatre I'd never experienced. Kent had been a religious-studies major at Yale where he also did theatre. So, it's not surprising that his Imaginary Theatre would create stories centered in spiritual themes.

The first original production of Kent's I was a part of was a theatre piece called THE SHEKINAH. The piece was a string of Jewish Hasidic tales told in Japanese Noh theatre style by six actors and one musician with ritual dances between the tales. Our costumes were simple—black with hats or babushkas and no shoes. The critics loved it and I loved it. I loved being a vessel for mythic stories told in a simple but unconventional way. I loved the silences the play created in the audience and onstage. It took me back to church, where at eight years old I'd stand on a wooden crate behind the pulpit and sing "The Lord's Prayer."

Next, Kent created a production of Kurt Weill's THE SEVEN DEADLY SINS with chamber orchestra. The theatre piece is a forty-five-minute symbolic journey of the Soul from birth to death as it passes through the Seven Deadly Sins. The narration is sung by a male quartet. The Soul is played by two actresses—Anna I who sings and Anna II who dances. They represent two sides of a personality—the

Ego and the Id. The Annas begin their journey leaving home together wearing a single dark cloak. As they move through the Sins of the world, the two sides of the personality begin pulling apart until they separate entirely moving through the Sin of Lust, where the Ego battles the Id. Then traveling through the remaining Sins, the two sides of the personality begin to pull back together until the Soul arrives home again as one under the same dark cloak.

At the end of the first performance the audience was silent for what seemed an eternity. We thought they didn't know it was over. We thought they hated it. But suddenly the applause came and with it the simultaneous standing ovation. It was an almost surreal experience. Atlanta audiences had rarely experienced this kind of theatre. And the critics praised Kent's work for a second time.

Next at Imaginary Theatre came Arthur Kopit's WINGS. It's the story about a woman in her eighties who in her youth had been a pilot and wing-walker. In the first moments of the play, she has a stroke and is plunged along with the audience into a frightening world where nothing makes sense. The play takes her and the audience on an internal journey through chaos toward clarity. In 1992 I would be cast as Emily Stilson in the musical version of WINGS adapted by Arthur Perlman and Jeffrey Lunden, to be performed at the Goodman Theatre in Chicago. The production would again play at the Public Theatre in New York, and Emily Stilson would change my life in ways I could never have imagined. But at Kent's Imaginary Theatre in 1980, I played Emily first at age thirty-three.

Imaginary Theatre's next offering was HOLY THE FIRM— Kent's theatrical adaptation of a book by Pulitzer Prize winner Annie Dillard. It is the story about a real event in her life living in Northern Puget Sound.

"I came here to study hard things—rock mountain and salt seas—and to temper my spirit on their edges" she writes. During her time in Puget Sound a freak accident occurs. A plane crashes. A little girl is struck by a flying piece of metal from the explosion and her face is disfigured for life. The book is about Annie Dillard's struggle to make sense of the event. It's her struggle with what kind of god would allow such random cruelty.

A friend of Annie Dillard's saw our production of HOLY THE FIRM, and asked how I'd managed to capture Annie so clearly. He asked how long I'd studied her. But I had never met her. He was amazed. So was I. I don't know how I was able to capture her. What I knew about Annie Dillard came from her words, from a couple of pictures of her, from knowing that she was a smoker, a wife, a teacher, and lived with a cat. But how she showed up in my body is a mystery. It's a kind of alchemy.

How is it that you rehearse for weeks learning lines and blocking, building relationships with fellow actors and the director, wearing your character uncomfortably, till one day she walks into the rehearsal room for you? She begins to speak for herself. And while you know it's a result of the work you've done up until then, it's always a surprise when she begins to use your voice and body. You've become a channel for her. It's a privilege to become someone else. It's remarkable. It's alchemy.

In THE SEVEN DEADLY SINS, I don't know how I was able to make a credible English translation. I'd studied German in college but I don't know where the skill came from to convert poetically from German to English. I believed that I could make a translation, so I did. Something in me knew how. Alchemy.

In WINGS, the character of Emily seemed to live already inside me. Kent had given me the role before he'd heard me speak her words. He had trusted me to play the role well, but when we auditioned young women to play Emily's therapist, he and I both were surprised to hear Emily's broken rhythms, using my voice already as if we'd been working for weeks. I somehow knew Emily. Or maybe it was that she knew me. Alchemy.

My work in all three of Kent's productions was born out of the fearlessness of youth. I was so full of "knowing," that I didn't yet realize I truly didn't know much of anything. But as I've gotten older, I have realized that the fearlessness of youth disappears. The only way to keep creativity alive, to conjure alchemy, is to cultivate a healthy curiosity.

Of course, it doesn't take much curiosity to imagine that the life of a theatre company creating alternative work, no matter how fine, might not be around for long. The audience for The Imaginary Theatre was loyal, but small. They loved the work like I did, but they weren't large enough to keep Kent's theatre going. Like Annie Dillard wrote in HOLY THE FIRM, "I came here to study hard things … and to temper my spirit on their edges," we studied the hard things we'd gone through with The Imaginary Theatre, the same hard things that Larry and I went through in Oshkosh and again with The Harlequin. So, Kent and I "tempered our spirits on their edges," and allowed The Imaginary Theatre to live only in the imagination. Kent let his theatre go.

Now I watch young theatre companies in the cities I've called home—Atlanta, Chicago, New York, Milwaukee. They begin just the way we began with high hopes and chutzpah. They struggle for two to five years to keep the doors open. They do new and fresh work, sometimes extraordinary work. Then finally they let go because doing the work along with making ends meet becomes not only physically exhausting, it begins to squelch creativity. Still, through the struggle, these young would-be professionals have begun to learn what it takes to produce theatre. And on the heels of their experience, some will decide which part of the craft to specialize in. Some will decide to teach. And many will leave the theatre entirely, because making theatre has been like spending time with a really good life coach. Making theatre in a company of their own making has given them direction.

CHAPTER FOUR

the alliance

*"The moral is Oriental ... accept whatever situation you
cannot improve."*

Hannah Jelkes, THE NIGHT OF THE IGUANA

The Alliance is where my work became my business. It's where I
became a member of Actor's Equity, the Actor/Stage Manager's
union. The Alliance is where working for a living became no longer
living primarily for the work. Acting was now fully my profession.

The Alliance was then and is still housed in Atlanta's Robert
Woodruff Memorial Arts Center, which also houses The Atlanta
Symphony. In 1962, one hundred three of Atlanta's most prominent
arts patrons were killed in the crash of Air France Flight 007
near Paris. So, the imposing gray stone structure that is The Arts
Center was built in their memory. The Alliance has two stages, one
downstairs that seats two hundred, while the upstairs main house
seats around eight hundred. The Alliance has since been refurbished,
but in 1980 the theatre's mainstage had a wide proscenium and the
house had a single balcony. The theatre felt larger than it actually was
because of the distance from stage to balcony. Throwing the voice to
the back wall of the balcony was a chore. But that was in the days
before miking became the norm. Now every production is miked to

some degree, even plays without music. Our collective ability to listen seems to have been altered by amplification. We expect it now.

Dressing rooms for the theatre are in the basement of the Arts Center, alongside a large common space. The common area serves as a shared "green room" with the Atlanta Symphony. And the green room is where we'd run into not only the symphony players, but the five cleaning ladies of the Arts Center who had been there for years. And those of us who worked at The Alliance many times knew them well. They were our friends. I remember the ladies—and that's what we called them, "the ladies"—worrying over me when I played the paraplegic patient in the play WHOSE LIFE IS IT ANYWAY? My character spent the entire play motionless in bed. One of the ladies worried for my health. "That can't be good for you Miss Linda. Anything I can do? You take care of yourself Miss Linda, now hear?" Sweet. The ladies were the first to call me "Miss Linda," which I've resented over the years. It has sometimes felt like condescension. But, from those kind-hearted ladies, I never resented being called "Miss Linda." I knew it was born out of affection, and the affection was mutual. They were a caring bunch of women. And wise. The Alliance never had a resident company of actors, but a few of us locals who were cast again and again became a kind of unofficial company. And the ladies thought of us as their own. We belonged to them.

WHOSE LIFE was the first time I'd work with my friend, Terry Beaver. Terry and I would play together a few times over the years, until twenty years from then we'd play opposite one another on Broadway in THE MAN WHO CAME TO DINNER. But at the Alliance in our first time together, Terry played the doctor to my patient. The role of the patient was originally played on Broadway by Richard Dreyfuss. In 1981, The Alliance brought him to Atlanta to play Iago in a production of OTHELLO opposite Paul Winfield. They were among the first famous actors to tread the boards of the Alliance stage. Also in the cast was the highly respected voice teacher Kristen Linklater, who played the role of Emilia and served as voice coach for us. Several of our "unofficial company" were in the production as well, including Kent and Terry Beaver. Kristen would lead us in vigorous vocal warm-ups. For one of those warm-ups, she took us out into the sunny day, had us hugging trees in front of the Arts Center, and releasing all manner of sounds while rolling down the grassy knoll outside the building. That day rolling down the hill with the others, I was squashed for a moment by Paul Winfield. He'd rolled over me. He was very apologetic. Truth is, I felt I'd been consecrated!

It was a bizarre experience working together with Dreyfuss, Winfield and Linklater—three very different personalities. Dreyfuss had a smart, combustible energy. Winfield's was lyrical and grounded. Linklater's was commanding but somehow distant. We locals all thought Dreyfuss's initial take on Iago was tremendous. In rehearsal he kept exploring, always looking for new interpretations. Whatever he came up with was fascinating and always true to the complicated character. But once the show opened, he continued to explore, which altered the shape of the performance show to show. He kept us on our toes. Paul was solid as a rock. His portrayal somehow made Othello's blind ego understandable, which is no small feat. He anchored our production. Soon after we'd opened, Paul's good friend Cicely Tyson came to see him do his work. Backstage after the performance, she praised her old friend, but told him in no uncertain terms that she was his one true Desdemona, that no one could ever play Desdemona to his Othello the way she would. She told him not to forget it. I wish we could have seen her one true Desdemona.

Paul Winfield was so kind to all of us. I'd acted with him one rehearsal day because I was Desdemona's understudy. Working opposite him was thrilling and at the same time comfortable. He was such a generous actor. I believe the world is less kind with Paul Winfield gone. One night after the show, I remember sitting at his feet during a party, watching him sip bourbon, a bottle of which always stood on his dressing room table. That night, I remember telling him through an alcohol-soaked blur, that I wasn't sure I could keep trying to make my living in the theatre. He said to me simply, "Then don't." It wasn't a casual response. It was an instruction. In my naivete I was asking him to tell me I couldn't leave the stage, that I'd be a loss to the theatre. Instead, he gave me a life lesson. I'm not sure I fully understood it then. But what it means to me now is that building a life is more important than building a career.

Years later when I was living in New York, I was given another kind of lesson while working out-of-town at the Alliance. I was doing a play called FRAME 312 by Keith Reddin. It's about the famous frame in the Zapruder home video of President Kennedy's assassination. I'd been invited to give a talk at a ladies' luncheon in a classy old home in classy old Ansley Park, which is one of Atlanta's most beautiful midtown neighborhoods. I'd been asked to talk about the play. I did my best to make it sound engaging which it was, but as a serious theatre piece not an entertainment. So, after we'd had our chicken salad and champagne, our lemon squares and coffee, the ladies moved to sit in a circle in the sunroom and listen to my talk. Twenty minutes later when I'd finished, the owner of the home asked if anyone had questions for me. An extremely well-dressed older matron with perfectly coiffed steel-gray hair had been sitting just outside the circle of women, smoking a slim cigarette through my entire talk. She spoke up and said that yes, she had a question, and in a deep upper-class Atlanta drawl she asked, "Now who is it that you are? And why are you here?" The woman in charge apologized all over the place to me, then said to the old woman, "You know why she's here. She used to be a star at the Alliance, and now she's on Broadway." There it was. I hadn't realized I was there to be a star, to play the Broadway star they imagined me to be. I had disappointed. My job that day was to entertain, not explain. They didn't want to know how I built my character. They wanted to know what it was like to be on Broadway. That's a lesson I still haven't quite learned.

So, The Alliance is where I began to understand politics. I'd lived outside communities for most of my life, never living in a city long enough to truly become a part of its community, and so I'd never developed a feel for my place within a community, except for a community of players. But even there I was not quite part of the community. I'd somehow landed at the top of whatever heap of players I was working with. I'd been given many if not most of my plum roles, and I know now that I'd expected those roles. As a young girl, I sang in churches behind pulpits, above everybody else. As I grew older, I expected to remain in that high position. I had worked for my position as a child, winning music contests and getting straight A's. My work had made me special to parents and teachers. So, I held onto expectations of remaining special. I'd been prima donna at home, at Wesleyan, at The Harlequin and at The Imaginary Theatre. Now thanks to Artistic Director Fred Chappell, I was to become first-blessed at The Alliance for a time.

I was given the crown almost immediately in my first mainstage role at The Alliance—Birdie Hubbard in Lillian Hellman's THE LITTLE FOXES. The local theatre critic gave me a full paragraph at the top of her review praising my work. This came on the heels of my having won best actress in a musical for playing Lizzie Curry in 110 IN THE SHADE at Atlanta's first theatre awards ceremony, the Atlanta Circle of Drama Critics, the ACDC Awards. With her review, Helen Smith, critic for the Atlanta Constitution, had marginalized Dana Ivey's powerful performance. Dana had held the position of first-blessed at The Alliance for years. I was the new kid on the block.

I was good in the role. But my performance was not so outstanding as Helen Smith wrote, for a few reasons. First, I was costumed beautifully with a lavender lace dress and dramatic black wig. But Birdie is a timid insecure woman who would have been better-served with mousy-brown hair and plain dress. Birdie has a dramatic monologue in which she shares her unhappiness, confesses that she's a drinker, then leaves stage in silence and alone. The audience applauded her exit every night. A mid-act applause. On opening night when the applause came, I was proud.

Now I know that I'd played into the "music" of the monologue, which was not right for this weak-willed character. But it was effective for audiences. I was doing what I knew to do. I "sang" the monologue and pleased the audience and accepted the applause and the over-the-top review as my due for a job well done.

But it was wrong for the play. And the review had not given Dana's powerful performance as Regina its due. Her mother, Mary Nell Santacroce who was then Atlanta's Grand Dame, gave me my first real lesson in politics. She congratulated me after the show one night, then said, "You know, you perform so well. And you have such a beautiful voice that I think of you more as a singer. Don't you?" Well. There it was. And she was right. Mary Nell Santacroce had complimented me and put me in my place in one fell swoop. She was letting me know that I'd have to work a little harder to earn my place in the Atlanta Theatre Community.

A year later, Dana Ivey would leave Atlanta and move to New York. She would stake her claim there as an actress to be reckoned with. Dana would create the role of Daisy in DRIVING MISS DAISY Off-Broadway. Years later in The Alliance Studio Theatre, Mary Nell would play that same role that her daughter had created in New York. Then years after that, I would play Daisy at The Milwaukee Rep as an out-of-towner directed by Kenny Leon who at the time was Artistic Director of The Alliance. Kenny was another Atlanta link in the oddly connected "Daisy" chain.

I would work with Mary Nell more than a few times while I was living in Atlanta, and came to admire her. She was a great actress, a teacher in more ways than one, and the ultimate "old pro." Dana and I were both living and working in New York when Mary Nell passed away. Dana asked me to sing at Mary Nell's funeral, and I said I'd be honored. It seemed right to be singing at the funeral of the actress who'd let me know I had a lot to learn about the difference between playing in musicals and in straight theatre. Singing for her memorial service, I felt like she was still telling me to stick to what I did best. I remember a time when Mary Nell and I were in rehearsal for a new play that she thought was "weird." During a break one afternoon, Mary Nell turned to me and said, "I like plays with a beginning, a middle, and a denouement!" And Mary Nell, wherever you are, I do too.

Thanks to Fred Chappell, then Artistic Director of the Alliance, I was given a slew of extraordinary roles in plays with a beginning, a middle and a denouement, by some of our greatest playwrights. Shakespeare's HAMLET was one of them, directed by Tony Tanner, whose claim to fame was as lead in the West End production of STOP THE WORLD I WANT TO GET OFF, replacing Anthony Newley. In Tony's HAMLET, I played Gertrude. Tony gave me one of the best pieces of direction I've ever been given. I'd auditioned with Gertrude's "Willow" speech telling the news of Ophelia's death to Claudius and Laertes. It's a long, poetical description, and I'm sure that in the audition I played into the music of the speech. Tony listened, then said to me, "That was lovely. Now do it again and this time deliver the words not for yourself, but for her brother, for Laertes." It changed everything. Now, whenever I have a big speech to give, I remind myself to remember not how I'm delivering the words, but for whom.

This was the second of three Gertrudes I'd eventually play. The first had been performed in 1980 at The Alabama Shakespeare Festival when its home was still in Anniston, Alabama. That summer I also played the first of my two Olivias in TWELFTH NIGHT, and my only Yelena in UNCLE VANYA. That summer playing rotating Rep is another of the high points in my acting life, and one of my happiest times in the work. There is nothing like playing rolling rep with a company, switching plays from performance to performance. The tragedy of HAMLET informs the comedy of TWELFTH NIGHT, informs the poetry of UNCLE VANYA. They illuminate one another.

And later at the Alliance there were more beautiful roles—Desirée in Stephen Sondheim's A LITTLE NIGHT MUSIC directed by Fred, in one of the most physically beautiful productions I've ever walked inside. June in Lanford Wilson's FIFTH OF JULY directed by Kent, a role against my "lady" type, who taught me something about discomfort and how to make a role your own without compromising the character as written. The first of two Mrs. Annas I'd play in THE KING AND I, which was a role I understood in my soul. This was a gorgeous production directed by Chuck Abbott who once said of me that I was a leading lady who didn't play the role offstage. I think he wished that I did. But that's another lesson not quite learned, and maybe never will be. I've never known how to carry myself in my personal life as comfortably as I carry myself onstage.

I've thought about the idea that we are all types, like maple or elm or pine are types of trees. Still, they're all trees. We're all people, but we're also types of one sort or another. And yes, we actors can play a variety of roles, but we can only play within the parameters of our given type. And I've come to think that our given type is a reflection of our essence—our particular spirit. Our spirit projects itself into whatever we have to give as people and as artists. And what I had to give as an artist during my time at The Alliance, could not have been given more fully than through the writing of Tennessee Williams.

At the Alliance I played four roles by Tennessee Williams-- Sister Woman in CAT ON A HOT TIN ROOF, Blanche DuBois in A STREETCAR NAMED DESIRE, Amanda in THE GLASS MENAGERIE, and in February of 1980, Hannah Jelkes in THE NIGHT OF THE IGUANA and Tennessee Williams saw me play her.

He was with us for a long weekend to see the premiere of his play, THE FROSTED GLASS COFFIN, which opened in the Alliance Studio Theatre downstairs, while upstairs on the mainstage we were playing THE NIGHT OF THE IGUANA. He arrived in Atlanta, as Scott Cain, entertainment editor for The Atlanta Constitution wrote: "... wearing a blue jogging suit, a coyote-fur coat and a pair of black shoes. He brought a razor with him and a satchel full of scripts—and that was all."

And one of those nights while he was with us, we threw him a party in Fred's candlelit Atlanta home with cornbread and coleslaw,

Brunswick stew and red wine. Tennesse had brought along an entourage of young men, one of whom kept his wine glass filled to the exact same level so that it seemed as if he never sipped a drop. I sat at his feet and listened to him tell stories of his life, and at one point he looked down at me, took my face in his hands and said, "My dear you should always be blonde." I had dark brown hair then and wore a blonde wig as Hannah. Then he said to me, "You know my dear, when you stand behind the mosquito net wearing your long flowing kimono robe with the poetry book in one hand and the palm frond in the other and the light is hitting your golden hair from behind, you look for all the world like an androgynous Madonna."

Oh my God! I was so flattered that I'd been able to realize the master's vision, because those words were nearly verbatim the stage directions at the top of act II that he'd written nearly twenty years before. So, I said to him "Well, you know Mr. Williams, that's what you wrote!" He raised his head, took a long pause, then finally exhaled and said, "Did I?"

I never knew if he was putting me on or if he truly didn't remember. Tennessee Williams said of our production in Scott Cain's article, "I think it's better than the original. It's more moving than the original." He also "heaped praise" on my performance and said "In a way she gave the best performance (that anyone has ever given) in the part. But I have to say," he added, "that Dorothy McGuire was equally as good." I like to say that Dorothy McGuire and I were the last two Hannahs he ever saw. Maybe I'm dismissing his praise as illegitimate because of the state of his memory at that time in his life. Or maybe I'm degrading my own performance as Hannah, but it doesn't matter. I think he loved all of us who gave Hannah her due, those of us he remembered. And I think I was lucky to be one of the Hannahs that he did remember with affection. I'm equally grateful to have it in print. The framed article hangs on my wall.

After our Sunday matinee of IGUANA that weekend, there was an audience talkback. Tennessee joined us and sat there in his Ray Bans and his blue jogging suit, his white Nike running shoes and his coyote fur coat. The audience was a sea of blue-haired ladies that day. And when someone asked whether there wasn't "a strong thread of Theology running through his work, a searching for God?"

Tennessee replied, "Theology?? What I'm looking for right now is a good-natured, reasonably personable chauffeur in Washington." At which point, a very enthusiastic young man in the back of the house stood up and said, "Mr. Williams. Oh, Mr. Williams, if you're looking for a chauffeur, I'm a very good driver." Tennessee took another of those long pauses, and said finally, "My dear boy, that is the very least of the qualifications."

He was then, in February of 1980, sixty-eight years old. Three Februarys later he would die at age seventy-one from an overdose of Seconal and alcohol. Some think it was suicide. I prefer to think not. He loved life. It was an unhappy way for such a great artist to die. I adored him. I loved speaking his words. I miss him in the world.

* * *

In the next years at the Alliance, Fred Chappell would hire Kent as his Associate Artistic Director. Kent would direct a show a year and would be in charge of the children's theatre programs at the Alliance. Kent would bring more diversity to the theatre hiring more actors of color, introducing mixed-race casting.

Looking back, I've realized that these years of the early eighties were a period of loss for me, in areas of my life that I'd come to think of as permanent, like youth, like being the Alliance leading lady of choice. Like losing my cousin Chuck to a cocaine overdose at the beginning of his career as a Broadway dancer. Chuck was from Judsonia, Arkansas, a small town his spirit was too big for. Chuck was the first boy I fell in love with when my family would take summer vacations in Arkansas and stay at Grandma Thomas's house. Chuck was a fish out of the water of small-town Arkansas. Chuck, when he'd made his first visit home from New York, shocked the cousins and aunts and uncles by sitting in Grandma Thomas's kitchen, in a wooden ladder-backed chair in the middle of her linoleum floor, wearing a white dinner jacket, crisp white shirt, thin black tie, black slacks, and slicked back black hair, legs crossed, smoking a cigarette, looking for all the world like Noel Coward. I adored him for his boldness and the joy radiating from his beautiful face. When I heard he'd died, I had my first experience of genuine mourning, of those waves of grief that roll up and out of you unexpectedly and surprise you when they come again. Chuck was my first real loss. Ugly way for a beautiful young man to die. I miss him in the world.

In 1980 I was thirty-three. In that one year I'd played Emily Stilson in WINGS, Hannah Jelkes in THE NIGHT OF THE IGUANA, Yelena in UNCLE VANYA, Olivia in TWELFTH NIGHT, Gertrude in HAMLET, and Mrs. Anna in THE KING AND I. I've come to think of 1980 as the signature year of my acting life, and a year of transition. Roles beyond this year began to come less frequently, which was disconcerting. Who was I if I wasn't acting? So, I decided not to wait for the next gem of a role to come along. I pulled out my violin, woodshedded myself into good-enough shape to join the Musicians' Union, and for the next four years, was a freelance violinist for whatever groups might hire me.

I played with the Atlanta Symphony in a concert conducted by Nelson Riddle. I played in the Concert for Prince Charles at The Fox Theatre, when the Prince was doing his American tour looking for his bride before Diana Spencer showed up in his life. I played behind Gladys Knight and the Pips, and Wayne Newton in that concert. I also did a Southeastern tour with British singer, Tom Jones. We were bussed every morning to the airport, flown to a city in the Southeast, played the concert, then flown home to turn around and do the same thing the next day for two weeks. I played in pit orchestras for musicals at the Alliance and Theatre of the Stars. This part of my life seems unreal, but for a time I truly was a professional violinist. Then I began to miss the stage.

* * *

A year or so after Kent joined the staff at the Alliance, Fred Chappell retired, and Kent was named Acting Artistic Director. The board of directors at the Alliance assured Kent that the search for a permanent artistic director was merely obligatory, that the job would be his. Kent would continue to encourage diversity at the theatre and hired Kenny Leon, the first African American to hold an artistic position at the Alliance, as Kent's associate artistic director. Kenny would one day himself become the Artistic Director of the Alliance and later go on to direct on Broadway winning multiple awards, including The Tony.

Kent began to cast me again. I was now in my late 30's, and so the roles offered were older characters. And I was uncomfortable with them, like the Miss Prism I'd play in Kent's production of THE

IMPORTANCE OF BEING EARNEST. 1985, we were in rehearsal for EARNEST, when I got a call from my old friend John Dillon, then Artistic Director of The Milwaukee Repertory Theatre. John Dillon had directed his first play, LITTLE ME at the Harlequin DC, when Larry and I were actors in residence there. John Dillon had called Larry and me to join the acting company of the Rep in 1976 when I'd chosen to stay in Atlanta, and Larry followed the call to Milwaukee. John Dillon had charged Larry with writing plays, had given him deadlines, and had produced Larry's plays first at the Milwaukee Rep. Three of those plays would move on to New York and one to London, and they would make Larry famous.

That day in 1985, John had called to give me the news soon after he'd heard it himself, that Larry had been killed in a plane crash. It was pilot error. The young female co-pilot was at the helm of a twelve-seater flying from Richmond to Staunton, VA. She'd misunderstood instructions from the tower, and everyone on the plane disappeared into the side of a mountain. Horrible way for a beloved artist to die. Even now thirty-seven years later, it's unbelievable. Larry was thirty-nine years old. I miss him so very much in the world.

When the call came from John, I asked Kent if I could leave EARNEST rehearsals to attend Larry's funeral for two days in Staunton, VA. He of course said yes. I imposed myself on the funeral gathering. I had stayed in touch with Larry's sister Jackie through the years, but I hadn't been in touch with Larry's parents since the divorce in 1977. I'd adored them and they had me. I wasn't sure they'd forgiven me for leaving Larry—Dolores maybe, but Percy I doubted. When you lose a marriage, you lose a family. I'd somehow managed to keep Jackie in my life but now I wanted this whole family back if they'd have me. The initial gathering with the family the day before the funeral was awkward. But I needed to be there with them. And over the next two days, as we mourned the loss of Larry, it came clear that they needed me with them too.

I stayed one more day than expected, three days in all. I'd called Kent the night of the funeral and said that I needed another day with the family. He of course said yes. But when I did come home, Kent was angry with me for being away longer than planned. I understood the frustration, that I was holding up the rehearsal process, but I didn't understand his level of anger. I thought he'd understood that I was going through a kind of loss I'd never experienced before. But he was my husband, and I'd been mourning the loss of my first husband. I can only imagine how he felt, but I don't know what his experience was. He didn't share it with me.

Larry and I had never lost contact with one another. He and I had exchanged letters and phone calls on a fairly regular basis and were the best of friends—maybe better than when we were married. Kent and I never really talked about my relationship with Larry, but here was an indication that all was not well with Kent and me. Our marriage had always been intense, but lately the passion sometimes became angry. And because we worked together the intensity grew. And because I was now working more for him than with him, my frustration grew. Larry's death and my reaction to it had exposed a growing crack in our marriage.

And in 1986 that crack was widened by a series of deeply unhappy events. Kent had taken a show to Broadway. It was called SO LONG ON LONELY STREET, by our friend and dramaturg of the Alliance, Sandra Deer. It was a new play that had started in the Alliance Studio Theatre. It was so popular that the next season Kent programed it for the theatre's mainstage, and again it played to sold-out houses.

Word got out about this highly successful new play in Atlanta, which brought New York producers down to look at the production. Respected Broadway producer Cheryl Crawford, one of the founding members of The Group Theatre, saw the play, decided to produce it, and said of it, "Maybe this is what New York needs." So, the play was taken to Boston for a Broadway tryout where the production was praised highly, and Sandra Deer was called the new Lillian Hellman. Then when it got to New York, the play was destroyed in the reviews. The response was shocking. It was most definitely unfair. And it was devastating.

Years later I'd have a similar experience when The Goodman Theatre's production of WINGS went to New York after a highly successful run in Chicago. It seems that New York critics don't like to be told what's worthy before they have the chance to judge for themselves. That may be an unfair or a naïve look at the New York critics' response to work that's been praised elsewhere. But we live in a country of many different cultures. What communicates in the South may not communicate in the same way in the North or the Midwest or the West and most certainly not in New York City. Values and sensibilities are different in different regions of our country. And, what a shame that still the ultimate legitimization of a new play seems to have to come from New York, and from one paper in particular, *The New York Times,* no matter how successful the play may have been before it gets there.

Larry's THE FOREIGNER had also been dismissed by the New York critics. Both Larry and Kent told me of their New York premiere opening night parties, that when the unfavorable *Times* review was read, people offered sympathy and said virtually the same thing. "We thought it was a good play, but I guess we were wrong." And the room cleared. Well. There it is. *The New York Times* can giveth, and *The New York Times* can taketh away. *The New York Times* certainly define-eth.

Larry had producers who found money enough to keep his off-Broadway production of THE FOREIGNER going until it found its audience through word of mouth and continued with a successful run. Kent was not so lucky. His very fine production closed soon after it had opened.

To add insult to injury, Kent returned home to be told he would not be made Artistic Director of the Alliance. He was told by the Alliance board president that he could of course, continue directing at the theatre, but that they were bringing in someone else with a "national reputation" to be the next Artistic Director, which ended up being a man who'd been Artistic Director of another regional theatre company whose experience was truly not national at all. Everything about this passage in Kent's life was unexpected and unfair and life changing. He told The Alliance he wouldn't be directing for them. He couldn't. He did a variety of things, but little money was coming in. I felt I couldn't work at the Alliance either after they'd virtually betrayed my husband. And without Kent's salary, my old fear of not having enough took hold.

I wasn't much help to Kent through his difficult transition. I remember a party that a friend of ours gave in great part for Kent, to get him out into the world. He'd been holing up, not participating. I remember watching him from a distance, sitting on a lawn chair, drink in hand, when an attractive young woman came over to him, stroked his back and asked how he was doing, and I saw the light in his eyes come back. I was at once jealous and grateful. I knew he needed a kind of comfort I couldn't muster because I was panicking about money. And I felt I was alone in searching for how to protect our future. I was operating in survival mode which sent me looking for acting work on the road, outside Atlanta.

I called my old friend and musical director from our Harlequin days, Kary Walker, who was now producer at the Marriott Lincolnshire Theatre in Chicago. Kary flew me in to audition for Harvey Schmidt and Tom Jones and their new musical of OUR TOWN called GROVER'S CORNERS. They cast me immediately as Mrs. Webb, and this would be the beginning of my life's next big shift. It was 1987.

unimaginable loss

Larry had been on his way from New York to Staunton, VA, where he'd just bought his Uncle Marvin's house, originally his grandmother Sally Shue's farmhouse. His plan was to turn the old farmhouse into a writer's retreat. Larry had just played Reverend Crisparkle in THE MYSTERY OF EDWIN DROOD at The Delacorte Theatre in Central Park. The production was on break between the summer outdoor production and its fall Broadway opening. Acting on Broadway had been one of Larry's longtime dreams. He didn't quite make it. And I've always wondered if my time on Broadway was in some way fulfilling Larry's dream.

The morning of Larry's funeral at the old Hebron Church in Staunton, Virginia, I found myself standing in Uncle Marvin's farmhouse kitchen making egg salad with Larry's sister, Jackie. She and I had gone grocery shopping earlier to buy food for the family get together at the house after the service. It was a glorious warm September day, sunny, with a crystal blue sky. And after the egg salad was made and the picnic tables on the back lawn covered with red and white checkered oil-cloth, I wandered through the house filled with Larry's moving boxes in various stages of being unpacked, remembering this knickknack, wondering about that one. I was drawn to a box filled with photo albums, and I began to cry almost immediately when I opened the top album, and saw us there—Larry and I on our wedding day.

I cried for his loss, for the loss of all that we had been, for the loss of all he could never become. Suddenly, I was shaken out of memory by what sounded like a bell playing a faintly recognizable tune. I dropped the album and called to Jackie, "What is that? Did you hear that?" She called back from the kitchen, "I don't know!" And then we heard a voice from the back of the house saying "Excuse me. I'm here to mow the lawn."

It was the gardener. He'd rung the doorbell. Larry's doorbell was playing the tune to Auld Lang Syne. Larry was telling us, telling me that "auld acquaintance should be forgot and never brought to mind." At least that's what I've chosen to believe.

At the funeral service later in the day, the minister made an announcement that the reception was to be at Marvin's house. Then Dolores, Larry's wonderfully exuberant mother shouted out, "Larry's house! It's Larry's house!" So, the gathering at Larry's house, filled with actors from the old Harlequin days, the Shue family members and New York friends, went on till dusk.

And all during the day when I'd walk through the dining room of the little old farmhouse looking through Larry's unpacked boxes, I'd notice the half-drunk bottle of single-malt Scotch sitting in the center of his heavy circular dining room table, and I'd think, "At the end of the day we Harlequin actors will finish his bottle with many toasts to Lars." But that didn't happen. And when the night came on and the only people left at Larry's house were his immediate family and me, there was a moment when I was rounding one side of the dining table and his father Percy was rounding the other side. Percy had not spoken two words to me during the day. He'd not forgiven me for leaving Larry, or for having had the audacity to show up at the funeral. But, as we rounded the table, he looked at the bottle of Scotch, then raised his eyes to me across the table and said, "What do you think?" And I said, "I think we have to." So, Percy would find his way toward forgiving me that night with many toasts to Lars as we finished Larry's bottle of Scotch, and patched our broken, caring relationship.

Two years from then I would be on my way to The Marriott Lincolnshire Theatre to do my first Chicago show, GROVER'S CORNERS. Larry's parents lived in a Chicago suburb and would see me play Mrs. Webb in that production. And from then until they would pass away years later and be laid to rest in the old Hebron Churchyard next to Larry, Dolores and Percy Shue were back in my life.

On Larry's tombstone is carved, "When it came time to give up childish things, he looked around, saw no one watching, and decided to keep his." It's from the first play he wrote for The Milwaukee Rep, GRANDMA DUCK IS DEAD, and it tells the story of his last year at Illinois Wesleyan, when he and his pals were graduating, heading off into the unknown future. I'm in that play too as part of his unknown future. We could not have known his unknown future would be so short.

CHAPTER FIVE

chicago

"The World is Very Wide."

Mrs. Gibbs and Mrs. Webb, GROVERS CORNERS

T he city of big shoulders put me to work the moment I landed and kept me working until I would leave six years later, platformed from Chicago to New York in a Goodman Theatre production of WINGS, the musical adaptation of Arthur Kopit's play of the same name. Now though, I was going into rehearsal for my first Chicago show at The Marriott Lincolnshire Theatre.

I remember my first day of musical rehearsal for GROVERS CORNERS. Kevin Stites, music director extraordinaire, who would eventually conduct on Broadway a few years down the road, was leading the first sing-through of the score. He was a wonderful task master. He demanded and got perfection from us singer/actors from the very first note. And I remember thinking, "This is where I belong." I needed the musical challenge of working not only well, but quickly. I needed the precision that Kevin was asking. It gave me structure. It stimulated and engaged the musician in me. And I loved it.

I was challenged even more, when Kary Walker asked me to replace actress, Mary Ernster, who was leaving the Marriott's current production of 1776 a week early, to go on to another job. Her role was Abigail Adams, one of my favorites. I'd played Abigail years before at The Harlequin so she was already in my bones. Of course, I'd be plugged into an already running production with different actors in a different theatre space, so it was exciting and scary to use those fight-or-flight muscles I hadn't used for some time. I leapt into 1776 and loved living inside Abigail again.

Here I was, my first weeks in Chicago doing what I did best, rehearsing in the day and performing at night among a Chicago company of players in a town full of working actors. I knew I wanted to be one of them. And to borrow a phrase from Ursula K. Le Guin, "I had come to where I was going." That's how it felt rehearsing with these artists in this city. And I loved it.

Harvey and Tom were not there only to observe rehearsals, they were part of the production. They were both in the show. Harvey was onstage playing the piano. And Tom was playing the role of The Stage Manager. I was the only other non-Chicago actor in the show, and so was housed in the Marriott Lincolnshire Resort alongside Tom and Harvey. We spent a fair amount of time together, we three out-of-towners. They were both originally from Texas and I from Arkansas with a Texan Grandma, and so there was a kind of simpatico among us. And for years, till he passed away in February of 2018, I was among those who received a hand-made Christmas card from Harvey. The cards tell stories of his childhood Christmases, and they are all works of art. They're hand-written using the same script that's used in the logo for The FANTASTICKS. Of course, they would be. It's Harvey's personal handwriting. I made a book of Harvey's beautiful, hand-drawn Christmas cards. I am so grateful to have it.

Tom and Harvey and I would share the occasional meal together, but mostly we worked. We rehearsed on the proscenium stage of an old movie theatre in Evanston, IL until we were able to transfer to the Marriott stage which is in the round. Entrances to the circular stage are from four voms, long ramps from the back of the house to center stage. Harvey sat onstage playing piano in front of the booth that housed the orchestra and conductor, Kevin. Tom as the Stage Manager narrated the story. He would walk the perimeter of the stage setting up scenes, sometimes joining the action as a character, making observations as he watched the story unfold along with the audience.

It's a unique experience for a Marriott actor watching the show from the back of the house before making an entrance. In large proscenium houses actors can watch the show from the wings, but it's a side-view, and often you can't see the whole stage. But at the Marriott, the actor can watch the play from the same perspective as the audience. She's in and out of the play simultaneously.

Tom had condensed the play to one act, eighty minutes without intermission. I thought Harvey's score contained some of the most beautiful music he'd ever written. While we were still in rehearsal, Harvey wrote a duet for Sharon Carlson and me. Sharon was playing Mrs. Gibbs and I, Mrs. Webb. The song is called "The World is Very Wide." It was a privilege having a new song written for us while we were building the production. The song is a lovely musical condensation of the "beans scene" between the two mothers in the original play.

The last twenty minutes of Harvey and Tom's adaptation from the wedding through the graveyard scenes was through-composed. It felt to me like a prose poem set to music. I'd been given a gorgeous hymn to sing that recurred throughout the play with its most beautiful version occurring in the graveyard, near the end of the play. Harvey's hymn transported me back to my young days singing behind the pulpits of Midwestern churches.

While we were running GROVERS CORNERS, Kent came to see me and the show, but he also came to meet with John Dillon, artistic director of The Milwaukee Rep who had offered him a job directing THE DIARY OF ANNE FRANK in The Rep's upcoming season. So, on a Monday off we drove the hour and a half to Milwaukee for a pre-production meeting with the staff and the actors of ANNE FRANK. I was part of the meeting as I'd be playing Mrs. Frank.

I sat among the others, many of whom I'd worked with, most of whom were Rep company members. I listened as Kent laid out his vision for the production. His presentation was very smart, and he delivered it well, but he seemed to spend little time getting to know those with whom he'd be working, or creating dialogue among the group. There was something uncomfortable about the gathering. Maybe it was I who was uncomfortable because I began to feel as if I'd be working for Kent again, and not with him. After the meeting we went to dinner, and over too many vodkas, Kent and I had a fight.

It was an ugly argument. I told him I felt he'd been condescending to the seasoned Rep actors. I told him I'd felt comfortable doing my work at the Marriott making money so we could pay our bills, away from the discomfort of our marriage for a while, giving us both space to heal our emotional wounds. John Dillon had been kind enough to offer work to Kent, and I told him I felt John's generosity wasn't fully appreciated. I told him that I felt personally unappreciated for having found work that was supporting us, for his not realizing that without the kindness and trust of my professional friends, Kary and John, we'd be flat broke. The blanket honesty of my angry words hurt

Kent, so much so that he virtually couldn't speak to me till after his flight took him home to Atlanta.

I didn't mean to hurt Kent. Of course, I didn't. I loved Kent. I was trying to show him the truth of our situation as I saw it, and how much it was hurting me. It had been two years since Kent's job at The Alliance was taken from him. He was still in a kind of mourning, a kind of limbo. At least it felt that way to me. I didn't know what to do but to continue looking for solutions to our situation, and that meant getting us both out of Atlanta.

Because of my job at the Marriott, and Kary's support, I knew I could continue to work in Chicago. It's such a theatre-rich town that I felt Kent could not only find work but make his own again. I felt he might create another Imaginary Theatre. Chicago was a place where I felt Kent and I could begin again together. But I know now that with that ugly alcohol-soaked argument, the crack in our marriage had grown to a fissure. The argument heralded the end of our marriage.

After GROVERS CORNERS closed, I went home to Atlanta to rest for a few weeks before Kent and I both traveled back to The Midwest to rehearse ANNE FRANK. And when the show was open and Kent went home, I stayed in Milwaukee to finish the run. On Monday's off, I drove to Chicago to search for an apartment where Kent and I might begin a new chapter of our lives.

I found one near Wrigley Field, a beautiful little newly refurbished apartment on the lower level of a duplex, with a back yard rimmed in lilac bushes. I felt like it could be home for us. I asked Kent should we take a leap and move to Chicago. He said yes. We put our house on the market. It sold quickly. Then after ANNE FRANK closed, I went home. We packed. We said our goodbyes to parents and friends. We moved to Chicago.

The day we arrived it was early spring. The weather was chilly, but the streets were filled with Chicago folk in shorts. Welcome to the upper Midwest. That day our street was closed off for a block party, and we couldn't get through to the apartment to unload our car. The moving van was to arrive later in the day. It was a challenge. I left Kent with the car while I walked through the party and found someone to help move one of the sawhorses so we could pull the car through the party and into the driveway of our new home. While we were unloading the car, we got a phone call from the moving company telling us the van wouldn't arrive until the next day. So, we finished unloading, locked the apartment, drove back through the street party, got on the freeway, found a motel and crashed.

We were almost through the transition. When the movers arrived the next day, we met them at the apartment. While they unloaded our furniture, we started arranging our life's things inside what I thought would be our home. Less than a month later, Kent would tell me as gently as he knew how that he was going to leave for Minneapolis and live there for a while. He'd felt comfortable, he told me, when he'd done a show there as an out-of-town director. And when I asked why he hadn't told me before we made the move to Chicago, he said he'd wanted to see me settled in the city first.

My God. He was trying in his way to take care of me, while I had been doing everything I knew to make life work for him, for us, for our marriage. The irony is that Atlanta was the first home I'd known as an adult, the only home I'd known, and I'd never have left had he told me he wanted us to live separately.

I'd been in survival mode for two years now and the object of survival was not just putting food on the table, but putting our marriage back together. I was determined not to fail again in a marriage. I was determined to "make it work." But I was trying to do it all by myself. And there was the problem. If we'd really heard one another, really talked, really begun to know who the other was, what the other wanted, what the other needed, we might have survived together. At the beginning of our marriage, we had adored one another. Our honeymoon lasted for two years before the reality of life as theatre artists kicked in with its inevitable financial struggles and insecurities. We were absorbed almost completely by whatever work we were making. We were living inside our work and not inside our marriage.

Kent rented a U-Haul, took one of our couches, the coffee table we'd had made to hold his grandfather's marble table top, various sticks of furniture, kitchen things and other pieces of our lives together. He loaded the rental truck, backed it into a car parked across from the apartment, got out to check for damage—none to speak of—left a note on the car, got back in the truck and drove out of Chicago. And though I didn't realize it at the time, drove out of my life.

I saw him once over the next year when he visited to spend a day, and to tell me he was filing for divorce. Then I never saw him again until years later when I'd moved to Milwaukee. He'd been hired to direct his second and only other play at The Rep. It was an odd, chance meeting. We had dinner together. He was changed. So was I. It was good to see him after those twenty-some years.

On the day he drove out of my life, I found myself with no friends in town but Kary, no work, and now no partner. With unemployment running out I couldn't process it all. I didn't know how I felt. But like Scarlett O'Hara in *Gone With The Wind* whose story I would one day narrate for Recorded Books, Inc., I couldn't think about it then. I'd think about it later.

I put one foot in front of the other, set up my apartment, discovered my neighborhood and called Kary. Next day, Kary called Rondi Reed at Steppenwolf who was in the middle of casting a show. I auditioned for and was cast in STEPPING OUT. I was offered the job the week my unemployment ran out. Saved, at the eleventh hour. And now, except for Katydid Kirkland McDougal, my sweet West Highland White Terrier, I was living alone for the very first time in my life. I was forty-one.

CHAPTER SIX

working actress

"Could I have done this? Yes, I remember the time."
Emily Stilson, WINGS

When I left Atlanta for Chicago, my actress friend Brenda Bynum gave me a lapel button that read "Working Actress." And now I was now discovering what those words truly meant.

I had been performing in the theatre all my life, but here in Chicago my relationship with the work changed. If I wasn't working, I was working to get work. I was auditioning more than I ever had, two or three times a week. Even GROVERS CORNERS and my Steppenwolf auditions had been, with Kary's help, given to me. But now I had to find the next work on my own. Still, in such a theatre-rich town there were more opportunities to audition than I'd ever had, and not only for the theatre but for commercials, television and film. Those genres were unfamiliar territory, so I had a lot to learn. I was challenged daily by this new city, by new people coming into my life, by this new work paradigm, and by living alone. Well, not entirely alone. I did have my Westie, Katy. But I spent so much time away from the house that I thought Katy needed company. So, I took her to the Anti-Cruelty Society on Grand Avenue to look for a friend. I found a big white and beige Buddha of a cat sitting in a cage. I asked if he could be put in a room with Katy and me. And from the beginning we got along just fine. We drove him home. He adjusted quickly. And we named him Charlie.

Now I could concentrate on work. My anchor was the theatre. And at Steppenwolf I was working in a theatre born from a company of players. This was work I truly understood. The show I was cast in, STEPPING OUT, was an unusual choice for Steppenwolf. It was hardly their signature gritty fare, but it was certainly an ensemble piece. The play tells the story of eight people taking a weekly tap-dancing class in the dingy basement of a church in North London. And we'd be performing the play in the dingy storefront theatre that housed the Steppenwolf Company at the time. The stage was not very deep, but was wide with a very low ceiling. It actually felt a little like a basement.

The audience entered the theatre from the lobby just off house right. It was a small house of maybe a hundred fifty seats, maybe two hundred, and the rows were slightly raked up from the stage. There was no other entrance, and there was no center aisle. So, during performance, if you were seated on house left and needed to leave for any reason, you had to climb over the people sitting in your row to exit to the lobby. Or, you might walk down the house left aisle to the small space between the front row and the stage, and walk to the lobby off house right in front of the entire audience.

One night some poor man sitting in house left got very sick, and instead of climbing over the people in his row, he walked down the house left aisle, stepped onto stage and behind the curtain where I'm sure he thought there must be an escape to the lobby, but nope. He threw up backstage while the play was going on in front of the curtains. One of the stagehands ushered him behind the set, passing by actors about to make entrances, till finally they reached the opposite side of backstage where he was able to exit to the lobby. Poor man. He was so embarrassed. And for the rest of the act, it was pretty smelly onstage, but as we say, "the show must go on," though I don't know why. Noel Coward wrote a song called, "Why Must the Show Go On?" But he forgot to answer the question. So, our show did go on while an intern mopped up the mess backstage, and we tapped our routines onstage in front of an audience wondering what the heck had just happened. Silly, really.

The production had a fabulous cast. Jenny Bacon, Shannon Cochran, Deanna Dunagan, Irma P. Hall, Celeste Lynch, Carlton Miller, Dee Noah, Ann Stevenson Whitney, myself and Francis Guinan, who was the only man in the show and the only Steppenwolf company member in the cast. The play at heart is about the relationships born among these eight people of different backgrounds, different ages and skills. They work together toward the single goal of giving one performance for an imagined audience, which when performed was, of course, for the real audience sitting in the house.

Steppenwolf company members are involved in every show they produce, and in our show, the two others besides Franny Guinan were Rondi Reed as director, and Terry Kinney as the lighting and set designer. We were visited from time to time by other company members. Joan Allen came to see our show and was very complimentary. Gary Sinise showed up to see the play and went out with us after to Chicago's historic Green Mill jazz club, which supposedly has the best jukebox in the city. I had a dance with him that late night. It was a heady experience.

There was a bar directly across the street from the theatre on

Halsted. And after performances, I'd belly up to the bar and drink bourbon alongside Tracy Letts. He was an actor then, and now is a Steppenwolf company member and award-winning playwright and film actor. I had no idea then what I was experiencing. Maybe you never fully understand your experience until you can look back from a distance. I had no real awareness of how important this theatre was and who I was working with. I was simply doing the work.

While running STEPPING OUT, I lost my voice for the first and only time in my life. I'd caught a virus that lodged in my larynx and took my voice for a day and a half. So, my understudy went on for one performance. I couldn't sit at home while someone went on for me. I had to see her do my role. I got out of bed, went to the theatre against the objections of the stage manager, sat in the back row and watched as this terrific actress, under-rehearsed as she was, played the role beautifully. She was really, really good. But then she would be. She was Jane Lynch. Yep, *the* Jane Lynch was my understudy. There's the difference between being a celebrity and not. In Jane Lynch's memoir she tells the same story about going on as understudy at Steppenwolf. But in her telling of the story, I'm "the actress who lost her voice," and in mine she's "*The* Jane Lynch." It's the way of our world.

There was another performance I should have missed during the run of STEPPING OUT. One night I was driving to the theatre in mid-town. I was heading East, and stopped at a four-way stop sign. There was a beer truck parked to my left on the southwest corner of the street perpendicular to my car. I thought I could see around it, but I couldn't and neither could the car sitting parallel to the beer truck on the cross street. As I moved out into the intersection, that car moved at the same time and hit mine broad side. The windshield spewed glass into the car. The driver's door bent into the driver's seat, moved the seat into the gear shift, and jammed shut. When the movement stopped, I had to free myself from under the steering wheel to be able to crawl over the gear shift to the passenger seat and out the front passenger door. Remarkably, I was not hurt. I was driving an old Honda with a steel frame. These were the days before everyone carried a cell phone, but the driver of the car that hit me was more than apologetic, sorry for what had happened, got me into his car, and called the police from his car phone. They came quickly, filed the report, and the other driver took full responsibility for the accident. I think the beer truck driver was fined for being parked too close to the intersection. My car was totaled and towed to a city lot. The driver who'd hit me asked if he could take me anywhere and I said, "To the theatre."

I told no one what had happened until after the show when I had to ask for a ride home. It was crazy now that I remember it. But I had a show to do and of course the show was all.

I felt only a little sore, but I'd tamped down any emotional reaction to the accident. After the performance, our stage manager was angry with me. It was careless and dangerous not only for me but for the show. I might have had a concussion. I could have passed out onstage. I had an understudy who had already proven she was ready to go on. Why didn't I tell anyone? I believe now I was embarrassed for having "done something wrong." I felt almost ashamed. Something in me wouldn't allow a stumble of any kind, even though what had happened was not my fault. The day after the car accident, my body was sore all over, but I never missed a performance because of it. Something in me wouldn't let that happen.

After STEPPING OUT closed, I was cast in the next show at Steppenwolf, RING ROUND THE MOON by Jean Anouilh. Again, it was directed by Rondi Reed. Again, the play was a departure for Steppenwolf. But it was chosen because of the talents of new company member, Tim Hopper. The play is a comic tale about wealthy twin brothers, Hugo and Frederick, who vie for the heart of a beautiful young woman named Isabelle. I played Isabelle's mother, and Tim Hopper played both Hugo and Frederick and was, of course, brilliant.

Opening night of RING ROUND THE MOON, I was introduced to the term "money player." Rob Milburn our sound designer was listening to the performance through a monitor in the upstairs rehearsal room. He heard laughter coming at a different time in the show than he'd heard before. He walked down to the theatre to see what was going on. The audience was laughing at me, at my character's antics. After the show Rob said to me, "I didn't know you were a money player." It felt like a condescension, like I was only playing for laughs. It bothered me so much that I had to look up the phrase, and what I found was, "A money player is someone who performs best under pressure, especially in a competition." Of course. The contest-winning, straight-A child in me had to win, in this case, as many laughs as there were to be had. Anything less was failure. So yes, I was a money player. I always had been.

me too

When I was in Junior High School in Pekin, Illinois, I was not only a straight A student, I was first chair violin in the Washington Junior High School orchestra. When I was in eighth grade, I broke my left arm trying to do a forward flip in gym class. Only a couple of weeks after the accident, I was back in the orchestra playing first chair with a cast on my arm. The orchestra's conductor who was also my violin teacher, had decided that since I could hold my violin up, and use my fingers, it would be all right for me to play with a cast on my left forearm. And my parents gave their approval. Unbelievable.

Orchestra rehearsal was the last class of the day, and at the end of rehearsal one day as the rest of the class was leaving, Mr. Keith asked me to come into his office. He was probably in his early forties, married, balding with one of those ugly comb-over hairstyles. He said he wanted to show me a new piece of music. He told me how good I was, how grateful he was to have me as his first chair, how he felt like he could talk to me, how beautiful I was, and how much he'd like to give me just one kiss. Then he put his hands on my shoulders, pulled me to him and kissed me. His lips were wet and they smothered mine. It was horrible.

I'd never been kissed before, and it scared me. I didn't know what it meant. I didn't even have a boyfriend. I didn't know how to respond except to leave the office as quickly as I could. Over the next several weeks it happened twice more, until I found the courage to tell my parents.

I don't know why I waited to tell them. I think I must have been ashamed of having done something wrong. I think I must have felt responsible for what happened, because along with being frightened and embarrassed, I was curious. On some deep level I took responsibility for his private wrong, because I was ashamed of my own curiosity. Still, I did break the pattern by telling my parents. They called him and told him to stop. He did stop. But he wasn't fired. I spent the rest of the school year in his classes, playing first chair violin with a broken arm. It was insane. Why my parents allowed me to continue playing in the orchestra, I cannot imagine. Why the school allowed Mr. Keith to continue teaching, I don't know. We didn't talk about it at home. I had no say. I was a child.

What would my life have been if those times after orchestra rehearsal never happened? If Mr. Keith had been a healthier soul and not taken me into his office, I might have learned to truly love the violin instead of feeling ambivalence toward the instrument. Playing the violin got mixed up in my developing mind with being broken and with shame.

I might have majored in violin in college instead of voice. I might have gone on to become a professional violinist. I might have been a teacher. I might have been a professor in a university, which might have given me a sense of financial security, which might have dissolved the ongoing fear of never having enough.

I had been taught to bow to authority, no matter how wrong that authority might be. Because of Mr. Keith's actions, my relationship with male teachers throughout high school and college was skewed. I felt I belonged to them. My parents' fear of authority was plugged into my young mind. I'd been taught to speak up, but not so loudly as to make waves. That was the lesson I took away. And there's a hidden message inside that lesson. It's about privilege. You are less privileged than he who carries authority. You are of a lower class. I think I took that lesson straight to heart and have spent most of my adult life trying to move beyond it. I thought something must be wrong with me. I was confused. And I felt ashamed. I was twelve.

CHAPTER SEVEN

winning awards

"Wow! This is the life, isn't it?"

Emily Stilson, WINGS

T he Steppenwolf productions gave me my first Jeff nominations. Chicago's Joseph Jefferson Awards are the city's version of Broadway's Tony Awards. I was nominated for best supporting actress in STEPPING OUT and our cast was nominated and won for best ensemble. Being in the Steppenwolf shows platformed me to other work, including two shows at The Goodman Theatre, Chicago's large regional theatre. In 1988 I was understudy to Carlin Glynn as Vera Simpson in a production of PAL JOEY, which also starred Steppenwolf company member Kevin Anderson as Joey. And in 1991 I played in THE VISIT, as wife to the mayor played by the very fine Josef Sommer, directed by David Petrarca. That same season, I played The Stepmother in INTO THE WOODS at the Marriott. And the season before, I had played Mrs. Alving in a beautiful but not quite successful production of Ibsen's GHOSTS at The Court Theatre. But the most memorable of productions I was a part of during the late eighties/early nineties, was STEEL MAGNOLIAS.

The show played first as a star vehicle at The Royal George

Theatre, and it was so successful that the producers decided to extend the run with a local Chicago cast. So, I replaced beautiful Constance Towers as M'Lynn, mother of the bride. Our production was directed by Pam Berlin who'd directed the original Off-Broadway production starring Rosemary Prinz in the role I was about to play. I would meet Rosie a few years from then, when we were both working at The Milwaukee Rep. Rosie has remained one of my closest friends for life.

Our local cast joined the run at the Royal George and then moved with the production to The Apollo Theatre where we ran for another six months. This was my first long-running show. We had a wonderful cast of women, including Vera Ward with whom I'd also shared stage in RING ROUND THE MOON, Nancy Baird, Mary Seibel, Brenda Varda and Rebecca MacLean. Rebecca and I remained close till our lives took us in different directions. Vera Ward was my good friend until she passed away years later. Her daughter Mari asked me to speak at Vera's memorial. Mari and I had met through the shows Vera and I did together. Mari, who is my age, is a gifted actress and voice over artist in her own right, and while Mari chose to marry and have children, I built a professional career. I took Mari's road less traveled, and she took mine. We've remained friends for life.

When Vera and Brenda left our show for other work, they were replaced by Roz Alexander and Kathy Hasty and the show transitioned smoothly. Someone asked during the run of the show, "Isn't working with an all-female cast tricky? Don't you have disagreements?" Absolutely not! Women are problem-solvers, and we know how to listen. It's not until a man is thrown into the mix that a natural competition comes into play. But in our situation, the only man in the company was our stage manager. We had two, actually, over the course of the run. Tom Joyce and then Steve McCorkle. Both terrific laid-back problem-solving guys. We Chicago gals felt comfortable in our guys' hands.

The Apollo's parking lot was underneath the EL, and every night there would be at least one car alarm set off by the rumbling of the trains passing overhead. We played through the city noise. It became a part of the performance. Something else became part of the performance one night during our run. Near the end of the show, at just the moment when my character, M'Lynn had reached the height of an emotional breakdown over the death of her daughter, I saw a man in the fifth row at my eye level, slump in his chair. The Apollo's house is on a rise, circling three-quarters of the stage and so steep it feels like a bowl. The man was partially lit by the spill of light from the stage, and I understood then what it means when they say someone looks ashen. His face was almost gray. I stopped and immediately called to Steve in the stage manager's booth, high above the house. He brought up the house lights and stopped the show. And I called out, "Is there a doctor in the house?" There was one. It was a good thing, because the man was having a heart attack. We actors waited along with the audience some twenty minutes or more for the paramedics to arrive and take the man out of the house on a stretcher. Then, as I'd been instructed, I asked the audience if they wanted a refund or should we finish the play. Almost as one, the audience said, "Finish the play!" So, we actors wound the play back to just before M'Lynn's emotional breakdown, and played to the end of the story. We got a standing ovation, of course, because the audience was completely with us for what we'd all experienced. And when the applause was done, Steve announced over the PA that the man who'd been taken to the hospital was doing just fine! There was another round of happy applause. After our cast got out of costumes and makeup, we streamed across the street to another convenient Chicago bar to celebrate, of course, with glasses of bourbon.

During this time, even with all this wonderful and varied work coming my way, I was beginning to realize that no matter how much I worked in the theatre, I'd never be able to make much more than it took to make ends meet. So, I began to consider trying television and film in LA. It was at this same time that John Dillon offered me roles for the entire 1991/92 season at the Milwaukee Rep. I would play Mrs. Gibbs in a sign-language version of OUR TOWN, Linda Loman in DEATH OF A SALESMAN, Mrs. Cratchet and other roles in A CHRISTMAS CAROL, and Poncia in THE HOUSE OF BERNARDA ALBA to be directed by Rene Busch, the artistic director of Repertorio Español in New York.

I took the offer. How could I not? It was an offer of a season's salary that would give me time to think about a move to LA, and with a season of incredible roles in great plays, working with a company of fine actors. Working with Rene Buch was a life lesson in itself. He was strong-willed and loved life. He had not chosen me to play Poncia. John Dillon had cast me for the season, and had given me the role. Rene was very clear with me from the first rehearsal that my qualities did not suit Poncia, the house servant I was playing. He pushed me to lower my center of gravity from my heart to my gut. When I finally found in my body what he was asking, everything changed—my voice, my gait, my rhythm. Even my thinking was somehow weightier. It was alchemy.

The play starred a truly fine actress in the role of Bernarda Alba, Miriam Colon, who was known in America primarily for her film work. She's now passed away. Rose Pickering was also in the cast. Rose was The Rep's premiere actress for many years. She has also passed away, and much too early in her life. Milwaukee audiences remember her as The Rep's Grande Dame. And she filled that public role with strength and grace. This was one of three times I would work with Rose—later that season in DEATH OF A SALESMAN, and years from then in a play called STATE OF THE UNION. But in none of those plays did we have scenes together. Actors truly come to know one another when we play together onstage. I'm sorry Rose and I didn't have that opportunity before she passed.

For me, DEATH OF A SALESMAN was as nearly perfect an experience as they come. It was a fine cast with Greg Steres, Ric Oquita, Michael Wright, Richard Halverson, Rose and Jim Pickering, and Kenneth Albers as Willy. Ken, as I write this years later, has just passed away after battling an aggressive cancer. He and his wife Cate moved through this passage with courage and a deep awareness of the preciousness of life, showing all of us who watched from a distance that death is only another part of life. Ken and I together in SALESMAN were somehow perfectly matched. We were both too young to play the world-worn Willy and Linda Loman. But John Dillon's production was a poetic telling of the tale, with only suggestions of solid houses and rooms behind us, and they came and went with such ease they might have been holograms. I remember what it felt like walking inside that imagined house on that stage in those lights. I remember what it felt like to scream when Linda heard Willy's car crash offstage. I remember what it felt like to kneel in a spotlight so far downstage center that the audience raking up from the stage three quarters around me felt like a forest-covered mountain, and I remember what it felt like when Linda's heart-wrenching last words to Willy in his grave, moved through me as she asked him why he did it. "I made the last payment on the house today. Today, dear.

And there'll be nobody home. We're free and clear...we're free... we're free ... we're free ..."

Ken was scheduled to direct EXIT THE KING at American Players Theatre, in the summer of 2018, but had to drop out because of his illness. He'd written a speech to deliver to the APT company members. In it he talks about having read EXIT THE KING, just before he went into rehearsal for our DEATH OF A SALESMAN years before. And he was reminded of something T.S. Eliot wrote:

> *"Time present and time past*
> *Are both perhaps present in time future,*
> *And time future contained in time past."*
>
> *"I cannot imagine the world without me."*

When I initially read those quotes, I'm not sure I fully understood them. Now what they mean to me is that past, present and future exist as one, that there is no imaginable world without Ken, because he was here, is here in memory, and forever will be. So will Larry, and Daddy, and Chuck, and all the others who've moved over into the time we cannot imagine.

John Dillon's production of OUR TOWN was unlike any other. He had hired deaf actors to play half the townspeople. The Webb family were non-hearing, and the Gibbs family, hearing. So, we Gibbs' spoke our lines, and when we spoke to a non-hearing character, we would use sign language as we spoke. When the non-hearing actor signed, another townsperson somewhere on the stage would voice for her, and likewise, if there was a scene between two hearing actors, then two non-hearing actors would sign for them standing in other parts of the stage. At all times, there were two languages delivering the play to the audience. It was wonderfully theatrical!

But even more wonderful was that this production was an exchange with The Omsk State Drama Theatre in Omsk, Siberia. Omsk and Milwaukee sit on the same latitude, and are sister cities. Hence, the exchange. While we ran our show on the Rep's mainstage in the Fall, the Omsk acting company had traveled to Milwaukee and were performing their play at the same time on the stage of the wonderful old Pabst Theatre, next door to The Rep. In the Spring, we would take our production to Russia, to Omsk to perform OUR TOWN for them. Then, in Siberia there would be not only two but four languages delivering the play. The Russian audience wore earphones and a member of their acting company translated. At the same time, two Russian sign language interpreters sat on opposite sides of the stage and translated from American into Russian sign language for the Russian deaf in the audience. When a performance was over after we took our bows, we were not allowed to leave until the audience poured onto the stage with arms full of spring flowers from their gardens to present to us. The flower I remember most is the lilac, Cyrien. I'll never see a blooming lilac without thinking of Siberia in the Spring. The entire experience was unlike anything I could have imagined.

1992 was one of the richest years of my life artistically, and I thank John Dillon for it. Sometime during the run of DEATH OF A SALESMAN, I began to question my decision to leave Chicago for LA. I was clearly a stage actress and this season at The Rep was reminding me who I was. My then agent and old friend from Atlanta days, Jim Carnahan had recently moved from New York to LA. He told me he'd represent me if I made the move. Jim Carnahan has since become one of the most powerful casting agents in New York, and the associate producing artist at The Roundabout Theatre Company. But in 1992, he was my agent. He had even arranged for a temporary apartment for me in LA.

My gut feeling was beginning to tell me that moving away from theatre in the hope of making more money in film was a mistake. So, I called Jim, and told him to let the apartment go. He was gracious. Then an extraordinary thing happened. Jim called me later that day to tell me that a casting notice had just crossed his desk and he thought I might be interested. The Goodman Theatre in Chicago was looking for a lyric soprano in her late forties or early fifties to sing the lead role in a musical version of Arthur Kopit's WINGS. Well. I hung up the phone and laughed out loud because I knew in my soul that this was my job. WINGS!

Emily Stilson had been my role since I was thirty-three playing her in Kopit's original straight play at Kent's Imaginary Theatre. Now someone had decided that Emily should sing, and soprano, no less. The role was mine. She was in me already. And I somehow knew in my bones that the show would play not only in Chicago but would move on to New York. So, I immediately called the Goodman, asked to audition, but told them that I had a tour to Russia coming up soon, and could I audition for them when I got back in the late spring? They said yes, that I was already on their list and auditioning in the spring would be fine.

When I came home from Russia, I called The Goodman again, and we arranged for an audition with director Michael Maggio whose life itself was a miracle as he'd recently had a successful double lung transplant and was now a completely new man. Jeff Lunden, the composer who played the audition for me, would become one of my closest friends for life. They hired me on the spot. What I did not know is that while I was in Russia, they'd auditioned others and had given the role to Beth Fowler, a wonderful New York actress. She'd taken the job but had recently backed out of the commitment.

So, in a sense I was their last best hope for finding an actress old enough to play into her 80's, and young enough to sing the challenging soprano role. And they were my best hope at platforming my career to a more prominent place in the business, where I might make enough money to no longer worry about where the next paycheck was coming from. At least that's what I thought would happen.

What did happen was that the production was praised in Chicago by audiences and critics alike. I won a Jeff Award, was given the Chicago Sarah Siddons Leading Lady Award. I was selected by the arts critics of *The Chicago Tribune* to be one of twenty-four Chicagoans of the Year in the Arts in 1992. Among the twenty-three others were Michael Maggio, my director, Eric Simonson and Oprah Winfrey.

David Richards, had been theatre critic for DC's *Washington Star-News,* and was my champion when I'd played all those ingenues at The Harlequin in the 1970's. He now wrote the Theatre View for *The Sunday New York Times.* And again, thanks to Kary Walker for being in touch with him, David made the trip to Chicago to see our production. He wrote a *Sunday Times* article with a picture of my Emily, arms outstretched spread across half the newspaper page. And the attention it got brought New York producers to see the Chicago production. One of the producers was JoAnne Akalaitis, then Artistic Director of The Public Theatre. She agreed to bring the show to New York in the Spring of 1993. And we came. Our entire production came. Our extraordinary Chicago cast—Hollis Resnick, Ora Jones, Bill Brown, and Robbie Lehman, all came. We all came with high hopes.

But the reception in New York was not what it had been in Chicago. Reviews were good to mixed but not good enough for the pre-planned move to the Helen Hayes Theatre on Broadway, once the show had closed at The Public. Those plans had included hiring an alternate actress to play Emily on matinees. The role was demanding to sing, at times almost operatic, and so it was decided that if we had an open-ended run on Broadway, playing eight shows a week, an alternate actress would play two of those shows each week. And the alternate actress they contracted was Rita Gardner, the original Luisa in THE FANTASTICKS. Talk about fantastic!

But with the lukewarm reviews, and the other actors in the show playing with a different lead actress twice a week, it was uncomfortable for all of us. Then unexpectedly the second week of performance, JoAnne Akalaitis who had brought us to New York was fired by The Public's board. They had hired George C. Wolfe to take over as Artistic Director a few weeks from then. To make things worse, with Akalaitis' firing, all advertising for our show stopped because we were part of her regime. And to further nail down the coffin lid of our production, the storm of the century nearly shut the city down for a week. Whatever momentum from word of mouth we had was squelched by this series of unfortunate unforeseen events. It was a hard introduction to New York show business.

I was bamboozled. How could a show be so praised in one place and virtually dismissed in another? But I remembered that both my husbands, Larry and Kent had gone through the same critical dismissal of their New York premieres. So, we were in good company. The rest of the cast was demoralized. We were all hoping for other New York work to come from our being seen in this production. But the play is a tour de force for the actress who plays Emily. And the other characters, albeit important, are there primarily to support Emily's story. This was a supporting cast of leading actors, all. And they were not able to show the breadth of their fine talents in these roles. They were bigger than the roles they were playing.

I think something else dampened the response to our production in New York. In Chicago's old Goodman Studio Theatre, the audience looked up at the play. The stage was higher than much of the audience. I was told by more than one person that at the end of the play when Emily dies, it seemed as though she actually flew out over the audience as the lights dimmed. In New York at the Public in the Newman theatre, the audience looked down on the stage and could see the stage floor. The production was "grounded" at The Newman, whereas in the Goodman Studio, the play floated. Emily's is a spiritual journey, so I think the theatre space itself in New York did not serve the play well.

At the end of our run, the other cast members eventually went back to Chicago. But I had a subletter in my Chicago condo, so I chose to stay. I was given an OBIE for my performance, which then opened up opportunities to audition for three upcoming Broadway productions—CAROUSEL at Lincoln Center, Broadway-bound BEAUTY AND THE BEAST, and DAMN YANKEES. I was able to find a sublet in Washington Heights for six months. It was in that apartment in The Heights that I decided to make a personal change to mirror the professional changes that were happening so quickly for me. I kept a journal at cocktail hour every night and talked to the various voices in my head that compelled me to drink. And over the course of a week, I found myself able to stop the habit of nightly drinking.

It was also in that apartment that I called my mother early one morning, and she said to me, "Oh, Linda, our Daddy has died." What? I'd spoken to her the night before. I'd seen him less than a month before when he and Mama and Lorna all three came to see me in WINGS, which would turn out to be the last time our whole family was together, the last time I would see my father.

In New York, Daddy had seemed tired but there was no indication of anything wrong with him. Truth was that he'd been diagnosed with an aortal aneurism that was growing. At the same time, they'd found a spot on his lung. And he was already living with macular degeneration. He'd decided not to have surgery or the lung biopsy. He'd had one aneurism ten years before and knew that his recovery from surgery at age seventy-six would take much longer than it had for the earlier surgery. He did not want to spend the rest of his life sitting on the back deck of his condo unable to even read.

My father chose to let go of what medicine might do for him. In making that decision he also chose to leave Mama with as much money as possible. He told neither Lorna nor me because he didn't want an argument. He would have gotten one. He knew that. He chose to leave the world on his own terms.

I flew to Atlanta where Mama and Daddy lived, and Lorna flew in as well from her home in Ohio. Her husband, Mark would join us later. We dealt with the business of the funeral and all the unexpected things that materialize when a person dies. Amazingly, I got through it all without drinking. The day before the funeral I got a call from New York telling me that I had been cast in DAMN YANKEES as Meg, the long-suffering wife. The role had happily been rewritten to be not quite so long-suffering, by wonderful Jack O'Brien, the show's director. So, there it was. My Daddy was giving me the job I needed to keep a salary coming for what would be a year and a half on

Broadway. Why do I say Daddy gave me the job? He always worried I'd never make enough money as an actor. But more important, I would spend the next year and a half at The Marriott Marquis in New York speaking my father's name to my onstage husband—Joe. My father's name was Joe. Magical thinking? Maybe. But I feel in my heart that Joe Wilson gave me the job.

A few years before, he'd also given me the directive to take care of Mama if anything ever happened to him, and it seemed that he'd arranged for me to have three months free to stay with her in Atlanta. Rehearsal for the out-of-town leg of DAMN YANKEES at The Old Globe in San Diego didn't begin until September. I still had the condo sitter in Chicago. I was graciously let out of my New York sublet because of my father's passing. I was blessed.

The morning after Daddy's funeral, Mama and I along with Lorna and Mark, had been invited to Mark's brother's home near Atlanta. They'd put together a morning-after brunch for us, complete with mimosas. So much had happened in the last month. WINGS had failed in New York. I'd been awarded an OBIE. Daddy had died. And I had been given my first Broadway show. So, when it was offered, I said, "Yes, I'll have a mimosa!" And it was lovely. Slowly, over the next few weeks, I was drinking again, daily.

* * *

I grew up in a non-drinking home. Oh, Daddy would have the occasional beer and there was a pint of bourbon in the kitchen cabinet for hot toddies whenever any of us was sick, but that was it. Alcohol never entered my life in an ongoing way until The Harlequin where we were paid in part with left-over food from the buffet, and all the booze we could drink. So, drinking after the shows was not only a company ritual, it was an ever-present comfortable way to come down from the extraordinary energy expended when performing at what I call the wrong end of the day.

Our bodies are programmed to begin relaxing late in the day moving toward sleep. But the performer begins prepping for performance in the late afternoon. Then after her show finishes at 10:30 or 11:00, the easiest and most available way to come down is to drink. And sharing the ritual with your fellow players, going over that night's performance, looking at what worked, what didn't, or what bizarre thing happened, is a joy. We're still working. We're processing what we did onstage that evening, and what we discover might find its way into the performance the next night in the subtlest of ways. Alcohol can serve as part of the creative process, the alchemy. But the body's tolerance for alcohol grows and so the more you drink, the more you need to drink to come down, six nights a week. And days off, alcohol plays a different role. It becomes a reward.

Alcohol had been in my life for nearly twenty years, since The Harlequin days, and had stayed constant through my marriages. Living alone for the first time in Chicago, alcohol became not only a reward. It became a partner. I began to rely on alcohol. Chicago was where I saw my first therapist.

That therapist was not much help with my drinking. When I told her how much I was actually drinking she said simply, "You gotta stop that!" But she did make me aware of something significant. She told me that I talked about myself in the third person. I'd call myself "she." "She had a one-night stand with this guy she doesn't even like." Or "She drove home on Clark Street at 2:00 A.M. seeing double." I was separated from myself, watching.

An Atlanta friend once called me "self-fascinated." She didn't say I was self-absorbed or self-conscious, self-important or selfish. She said "self-fascinated." And now that made sense. I was living outside myself, observing my own behavior. It resonated with the child in me who was fascinated by her own talent, amazed that she had a voice that could silence a room. Maybe I'd always been floating above my life watching as it unfolded. I think I had been. When I was in second grade in Pekin, Illinois, I remember walking home from school along with all the other children. But I wasn't among the others, I was above them looking down. I was flying, or more like gliding on a cushion of air, my own magic carpet about twenty feet above the others. Maybe it was a dream. Probably. But then maybe not. Magical thinking? That memory is very strong.

Maybe I was removed from the others and never felt I belonged because of all the moves in my childhood. But whatever the truth of that memory, I do believe that watching my life from a distance was a form of self-protection. Against what, I'm not sure, but what is clear is that the only safe place, the only place I was comfortable in my own skin was onstage. The stage was, as John Guilgud has called it, "home." On stage, I was home. I still am.

When I performed, I was discovering who I was by interpreting other people's words. But in the real world I didn't know so clearly who I was, who to be. So, I'd jump outside of myself and observe. But after the show I could let go even the observing, and hide from myself. I disappeared behind the alcohol.

Was I an alcoholic? Certainly, I drank too much, but so did everyone else I worked with. I might have been called a functioning alcoholic because overdrinking never got in the way of my work or seeking the next work. But it was self-destructive in physical and emotional ways. And it showed itself most in the isolation I experienced even as I drank with others after performances. It was a spiritual isolation. I didn't know that then. I was maintaining a balance so that I could do my work, and alcohol helped me to keep that balance. Or so I thought. Truth is, there was no balance. My life was about working, or working to generate more work. My energy was entirely focused on performing and survival, from show to show. I was doing what I thought I had to do. It never crossed my mind that I might stop performing, that I might look for ways to create a kinder life for myself.

* * *

After Daddy's funeral and a quick trip back to New York to gather my things and turn in the keys to my Washington Heights sublet, I drove to Atlanta to stay with my mother during the warm summer months of 1993. It was familiar territory being with Mama. We'd spent so much time alone together those first seven years of my life before my sister Lorna was born. Living with her for the first time in what had to be forty years, felt oddly as if no time had passed. I slid into the familiar role of Mama's girlfriend.

And we did girlfriend things that summer. We bought clothes. We talked. We went to movies. We went out for meals because neither of us liked to cook. Sometimes we were joined by her friends, the wives of the old guys in Daddy's golf club. We'd lunch at favorite Atlanta restaurants; The Colonnade, or the famous Mary Mac's Tea Room, or any one of the Piccadilly Cafeterias in town where you could choose your meal from a plethora of Southern comfort foods. There's no Northern version of those good ol' Southern cafeterias.

I was home. This was not my parents' home, but mine. They'd

moved to Atlanta after their retirement move to Arkansas, their childhood home. And when they found that "you can't go home again," they'd moved to live near me. My sister had done the same a few years earlier when her second marriage had ended. I'd become a kind of anchor for my family. Or it seemed that way to me. But now I was back in the home I never would've left if I hadn't made what I thought was the necessary move to Chicago to save my marriage. Atlanta had been home in my coming-of-age days, then again during my prime years on the stage. I was home in Atlanta having a lazy summer vacation. And when Mama took her afternoon naps, I'd take walks on a nearby dirt road flanked by Blackberry bushes, accompanied by dragonflies the size of hummingbirds.

That summer was a gift for both Mama and me, a respite before we each moved on to the next part of our lives. But it was also the beginning of a shift in our relationship. I was certainly her best friend. I had always been a source of pride for Mama, often her showpiece which was sometimes OK with me, sometimes not. But now, I was becoming something more for her. I was beginning to fill Daddy's shoes. I was becoming my mother's partner.

survivors

Mama was born Bessie Lorene Thomas in Russell, Arkansas, population 172, on Halloween, 1921. Her parents, Harriet Elizabeth Fowler and Shelby Jay Thomas were farmers, and their house was at the end of a long dirt road running alongside a railroad track.

Joseph Carr Wilson, my Daddy, had seen Mama for the first time when her brother Leonard brought him to their farmhouse home to help at strawberry-pickin' time. One morning Daddy came down the attic stairs, saw Mama standing over the kitchen stove, and thought she was the most beautiful woman he'd ever seen.

Three years later, in 1945, Daddy came home from serving in the army in WWII. His unit had been attached to the Marine Americal Division which was the first to storm the beaches of Guadalcanal in the South Pacific. And after he healed from the trauma and the malaria that came home with him, he married Bessie Thomas.

Before the war Daddy had worked at Mr. Butler's shoe store in Jonesboro, Arkansas, his hometown. After the war, he went to work in the repair shop at the back of Mr. Butler's store, and there he learned the cobbler's craft. The owner of another shoe repair shop in nearby Newport had somehow heard about Joe Wilson, and offered him a job. So, Joe and his new wife Bess—Mama would never call herself Bessie again—moved to Newport. A year later, on December 19, 1946, I was born in Newport, Arkansas.

We lived in a duplex across from a Dr. Pepper plant, but in only a few months we moved to a larger duplex when I wasn't yet one. It was the first of many moves, the beginning of a way of life that would continue throughout my life. It was a kind of training for the freelance actor I would one day become.

Our next move was to Judsonia, Arkansas. We lived in an apartment over a funeral home, and shared a deck with the family living in another apartment on the second floor. Mama told me those folks loved me so much that if she'd wanted to, she could've given me away. I have a notion she may have been tempted.

We moved next to a furnished apartment in another duplex in Judsonia. The house had a big garden in the back yard. Mama told me we ate primarily from that garden. The owner of the house loved talking to my Daddy who had the gift of gab. He'd ask Daddy to "Come on over and gas with me for a while." So, in the evenings they'd sit in the rockers on the front porch and gas away until suppertime. I'd sit on the porch steps and listen. Their voices sounded like music to me. Now, I was two.

The next move took us to Bald Knob, Arkansas, and a boarding house with three apartments and a shared kitchen with a dozen other tenants. Living with so many people scared me, and I remember hiding inside a dark closet off the kitchen, watching them all from a distance through the partially opened door. Daddy had bought shoe repair equipment by then, and found space to set up a shop in a Western Auto building across the street from the boarding house. With the help of a neighbor, Daddy built a three-room apartment onto the back of his new shoe shop, and it became our own little home. Mama told me we had to share the bathroom with the Western Auto store, but I find that hard to believe. I don't remember much about that apartment. I do remember hiding under the porch of the house across the street, looking through the crisscross slats at people going in and out of the Western Auto Store. All those people coming and going so close to my home scared me. But sitting on the cool dirt floor, watching from a distance, I felt safe. I also felt safe inside Daddy's shop, with its comforting smells of leather and rubber cement, and the Cat's Paw emblem on the window watching over me. I would sit on the floor behind the counter and teethe on rubber heels. Now I was three.

Daddy slowly began to realize he'd never make enough money to support a family with his repair shop in this small Southern town. So, he sold his shop with the equipment, and also the apartment he'd built. "Lock, stock and barrel." he said. Then he piled everything my parents owned, along with the baby bed and me, into a car he had bought with proceeds from the sale. He moved us north in search of work at Caterpillar Tractor Company in Peoria, Illinois. I was four years old.

We lived in North Pekin, across the Illinois river from Peoria and the Caterpillar Tractor plant where Daddy had been hired. Our new home was a little four-room wood-frame house with a basement and a back yard. It felt huge. Daddy looked for work daily in Peoria, and applied at a wholesale leather company owned by a man who also had several warehouses in Illinois, Iowa and Indiana. Daddy was hired by Mr. C. V. Engstrom part time, while continuing to work full time at Caterpillar. After only a few months, Engstrom saw Daddy's potential and hired him full time for an opening in Springfield, Illinois, as manager of Engstrom's warehouses.

Mama and I stayed in North Pekin while Daddy lived in a hotel in Springfield and would come home weekends. Daddy was Engstrom's trouble shooter, and during the week he'd travel from Springfield to the Southern Illinois and Indiana warehouses. We'd visit Daddy occasionally and stay with him in the hotel. At night, I remember the red neon sign outside the hotel room window blinking on and off while I lay awake. It seemed unreal, like something from a movie.

We went to a lot of movies, or rather we went to "the show" as my parents called it. And when they were deciding if they could afford to go to the show, they'd spell it out. "Do we have enough cash for the S-H-O-W?" I learned early on what "S-H-O-W" meant. So I would ask "Can we go to the H-O Dubby?" I loved the H-O Dubby. I loved getting lost in the big beautiful faces on the screen. I felt what they were feeling. I disappeared into their worlds. By now I was five.

Mama and I soon moved to be with Daddy in Springfield, and the three of us lived in a studio apartment with a Murphy bed and a small kitchenette. It was only one big room, but it was close to Stuart School where I would begin first grade. I did love school, but here at Stuart, I received my first artistic criticism. My favorite dress was chocolate brown and black plaid with a white bib. It went perfectly with my favorite chocolate brown coat. Our first-grade teacher gave an assignment to color in the Christmas symbols alongside a story we'd written. I colored my Christmas tree chocolate brown and the stars black with white stripes. The teacher was put out with me. She kept me after class and made me do my story again, changing my colors to red and green. She didn't understand that I'd used the colors of the little plaid dress that I loved. I didn't understand why she was angry. I thought I'd followed the rules. I'd colored inside the lines. But it was clear that I had done something wrong. And I felt ashamed.

Soon after we'd moved to the studio apartment, Daddy's older brother Herb lost his job in Arkansas. Daddy invited his big brother and his wife and their two daughters to come live with us in Springfield. Now we seven bunked in the studio apartment. But it was only for a few weeks until Uncle Herb found work. So, we all moved to an upstairs duplex apartment in downtown Springfield. It had a living room, a kitchen, two bedrooms, and a screened-in back porch. It felt palatial. The brothers probably chose to keep the families together to save money. My father had chosen not to take advantage of the G.I. Bill when he left the army which would have helped with a low-cost mortgage, or given him a grant to go to college. Daddy had left high school after the tenth grade, which wasn't unusual at that time. Maybe he was embarrassed to ask for money to finish high school. Whatever the reason, he'd told Mama that he'd done his duty in the war, and taking the government's money because he'd simply done his job seemed like receiving a handout. Daddy's high principles stood alongside his sometimes-poor judgment.

But I imagine the more important reason we all stayed together was that Daddy and Uncle Herb were best friends. They both had families now. Both were just starting out. They leaned on one another for moral support. And they enjoyed one another. I watched the two of them in the linoleum-tiled kitchen sitting at the big round table talking and laughing over their beers, or playing canasta with Mama and Aunt Catherine with her ever-present cigarette and her high-pitched laughter. I played on the porch with my cousins, Mary Ann and Sandy, drawing pictures with crayons on big pieces of butcher paper, or listening to the radio over the rolling laughter from the adults in the kitchen. Laughter was a huge release for my family. Most of the time what they laughed about seemed silly to me, and very loud. So, I'd walk into the kitchen where the adults were sitting around "gassin' and laughin.'" And I'd sing all the verses of "Silent Night" again, until the room became quiet. It's the only way I could get any attention from this noisy family. It's also when I began to understand that there was power in my voice. I was six.

A year later, Daddy was transferred to Rockford, Illinois to help close a small warehouse. So, we left Herb's family in the Springfield apartment, and my parents bought our first trailer, a little silver job called "The New Moon" and towed it to Rockford. Up until then we'd lived in furnished apartments in people's homes, because apartment houses in larger numbers were only beginning to be built. After WWII, living in trailers was not uncommon. Trailers were "starter homes."

I remember being alone with Mama in the New Moon when Daddy was away. I'd wake in the middle of the night, and get out of bed. I'd go to the front door of the trailer, and check to make sure it was locked. I'd do that nearly every night while he was gone, because I was afraid. And if I was afraid, I imagine that my mother was afraid too. I'm sure I took her fear with me to the door to make sure we were safe, locked inside, protected while Daddy was gone. I carried my mother's fear. I think maybe I still do.

Within the year, the Rockford warehouse was closed, and we moved again, this time to an in-town trailer park in Pekin, Illinois, across from a Spudnut shop. We had too many breakfasts of those delicious sugary potato-flour donuts. I went to second grade at Wilson school. And it was here that my sister Lorna was born when I was seven.

When I was eight, Daddy was called by Engstrom to move us to Des Moines, Iowa, to manage the warehouse there. And here my parents bought "The Commodore," a large trailer with two bedrooms, living room, kitchen and bath. I went to third grade at Madison elementary school, which is where I made my first friend, Mary. She and I would watch the other kids and talk about them, like the pretty blonde girl named Elaine who fainted in class one morning and had to be revived by the teacher, who then praised Elaine for her courage. But Mary and I knew that Elaine had pretended to faint to get out of taking a test. Stupid teacher. Mary and I could see through people. At least we thought we could. We were studying character.

One day, my parents asked me what nationality my friend was. I believe now that Mary was mixed race with her coffee-and-cream-colored skin and light brown tightly-curled hair. I thought she was pretty. When I asked, she told me she was American, and then after she told her mother what I'd asked, she was never allowed to play with me again. I don't know if my parents were prejudiced or not. But I know now that I lived my early years in all-white neighborhoods in Illinois and Iowa, and I was born out of the all-white small towns in Arkansas. Pekin, Illinois was a nearly all-white town, and my parents had chosen to live in Pekin even though my father worked in Peoria, which at the time had a population that was one third black. I don't remember meeting any black person before Mary, assuming she was black. I had no impulse to wonder about her race. I just saw Mary. My parents may have been only curious, but now, I realize the question itself is suspect. Mary's mother was insulted. I thought I'd done something wrong, and I felt ashamed.

After the school year, my parents moved us to Oak Park Trailer Park which was much better groomed than the park we'd just left. But I wonder now if we moved because there were people of color living in the park that made my parents uncomfortable. There'd been a family of carnival people living there, and I'd watch as the children practiced juggling with bowling pins and balls and rings. I was amazed by their father walking on his hands up and down the dirt park paths. I'd watch them working on their skills for hours. I broke my arm for the first time doing a forward flip, trying to imitate the carnival people. I was trying to develop my own skills.

There was a wonderful open prairie of grasses next to that trailer park, where I would escape to sit by myself and make clover chain necklaces, and hold grasshoppers in my hand until they spit their "tobacco juice" on my palm while I lay on the grass brushed lightly by a gentle breeze. Communing with nature, sitting in fields, I was learning to meditate.

One day an ancient turtle showed up and sat motionless on a dirt path in the trailer park. It was huge, at least a yard from nose to tail. No one knew where it came from, and the stillness with which it sat on the path was at once disturbing and calming. Someone said that the park had been built on what was once a swamp, and that the turtle had probably come home to die. It carried with it a mystery that moved me. But we left the park before I found out what happened to the turtle. I was fascinated by it, and by the park whose name I never knew. It had opened me to people and worlds different from the small safe one my parents had built for Lorna and me.

But I was a child and adjusted quickly, and found another friend once we'd moved. Kathy Crone and I would sit on swings in the Oak Park Trailer Park playground and sing "Tonight, You Belong to Me." Or "Volare" that I especially loved singing. It conjured the exotic places I'd seen on screen at the "H-O Dubby." And I remember getting lost for hours watching our first TV, a tiny little Motorola. I'm sure I learned how to play comedy from Sid Caesar's Your Show of Shows. I went to fourth grade at the Julia Ward Howe School. And, when recruiting began for young musicians, I asked my parents for a piano. I got a violin. They told me a piano wouldn't fit into our trailer. Now I was nine.

Then when I was ten, Daddy was called back to Engstrom's main store in Peoria where he was now the boss's right-hand man. We lived again at the in-town trailer park in Pekin and ate more Spudnuts. I went back to Wilson School for sixth grade. Daddy's new position came with a larger salary, so my parents were able to come up with a down payment on a little two-bedroom house on top of a hill where they would live until their retirement. I'd live there through my junior high and high school years. In all our moves to Pekin, Springfield, Rockford, Des Moines and Pekin again, we found churches to attend. And I would sing solo hymns in every one of them. It was my joy. And I shared that joy, singing behind the pulpits of Midwestern Baptist Churches. But it was more than my joy. It was my job. I was following my parents' lead.

Mama and Daddy were natural salesmen. They had a great sense of style. They knew how to dress. They had beautiful dark hair and eyes and ready smiles. They were great performers in "the real world." So, I performed too. I felt an early responsibility to help put food on the table. But Mama and Daddy had a kind of faith that money would be there when it was needed. And it always seemed to show up, usually at the last minute. There was a time when Daddy found a wallet on the street with no ID, and just enough cash for us to make it through the week. So, along with the fear of not having enough, I was developing a belief that something would come along at the eleventh hour to save us. It was belief in a kind of magic, or a strong sense of faith. Maybe a little of both. I wasn't the salesman my parents were. But I could move people with my voice. I was learning how to play an audience, singing for my supper.

In 1964 when I was seventeen, my parents took out a loan to send me to the School of Music at Illinois Wesleyan University where I would study voice and violin. In 1968, I would graduate Magna cum Laude with a Bachelor of Music in Voice. Then over the next twenty-five years I would continue moving to twenty more apartments in nine different cities, until DAMN YANKEES went into rehearsal in San Diego in 1993.

back to work

"You gotta have heart!""

The Washington Senators, DAMN YANKEES

In September of 1993, Katy dog, Charlie cat and I left my mother's home, and made the temporary move to San Diego, California. We would be there for the three months it would take to rehearse, finesse, and preview DAMN YANKEES before its eventual opening on Broadway in February of 1994.

DAMN YANKEES is a musical about Joe Boyd, the middle-aged fan of the fictional Washington Senators baseball team. Joe would sell his soul if only the Senators could beat the New York Yankees and win the pennant. Enter the Devil, disguised as Mr. Applegate, who offers to turn Boyd into Joe Hardy, a powerful young baseball player, in exchange for his soul. When Boyd agrees, he's transformed into young Hardy and leads the Senators on a winning streak. But when Joe begins to miss his wife, he takes a room in their home as a boarder. Applegate sends the temptress Lola to convince Joe to come back and lead the Senators to victory. Joe has a crisis of spirit which miraculously allows him to have his cake and eat it too. He wins the pennant for the Senators at the eleventh hour, just as he's being turned back into Joe Boyd and comes home to his beloved wife. I was playing the beloved wife, Meg.

Our theatre was The Old Globe, San Diego's large regional theatre where at the time, our Tony Award-winning director Jack O'Brien was artistic director. DAMN YANKEES was part of the theatre company's six-play Festival, from June through November.

We arrived, most of us from New York, to be housed in several apartment complexes. It was a large cast—twenty-three including swings and standbys. Those among us I remember being housed in my complex were Victor Garber, our Devil, Susan Mansur who was playing Meg's sister, Scott Wise our Tony-award-winning lead dancer, Greg Jbara, our catcher, Vicki Lewis, the nosy newspaper reporter, and Dick Latessa, our coach. Beloved Dick Latessa who's now passed away, was charged with leading the ball players in singing maybe the most recognizable song from DAMN YANKEES, "You Gotta Have Heart!" And Dick's heart was big enough to carry that message for all of us.

The first day in the Old Globe rehearsal room, I was again walking in unfamiliar territory. When I entered the room filled with New York musical theatre singer/actor/dancers, this huge, visceral, extroverted, loud energy nearly knocked me over. I was overwhelmed.

I gravitated toward Susan Manser who was playing my sister, and whose slightly Texas accent made me wonder if that was why Jack cast us as sisters, both of us born in the South. I remember meeting the other introvert Jere Shea, who was playing our young Joe Hardy. I began to relax, knowing I wasn't alone in this room full of energetic actors. And there was also Dennis Kelly with his golden singing voice, who was playing the older Joe Boyd. Dennis and I hadn't met even though we were both Chicago-based actors. Dennis told me later that he had seen me play in WINGS at the old Goodman Studio, and had said to his partner Ami, after the performance, "I'm going to work with her someday." He somehow knew.

One of the most beautiful moments in the production was a trio created by our wonderful musical director James Raitt, cousin to singer John Raitt and his daughter Bonnie. James had adapted the song "Near to You," that in the original production was a solo sung by young Joe to Meg. In the newly created trio, Meg was alone in her bedroom hearing the voices of both young and old Joe, as they all three sing the close harmony of the trio. It was a beautiful musical adaptation of the rewritten scene, thanks to both Jack and James.

There was a time during rehearsals when we nearly lost James' beautiful musical version of the trio. Our composer, Mr. Richard Adler who was with us during much of rehearsal, felt that the harmonies in the adaptation were too modern. Jack convinced him, not without some cajoling, to allow us to keep most of James' version, but not all. The chords over the final word of the trio still move from dissonance to harmony, but what James had originally written was much more complicated, more extended, and made the final resolution even more beautiful. Still, the trio is one of the most unusual treatments of a song in musical theatre. And later, when we opened on Broadway, John Simon wrote in his *New York Magazine* review that the trio "is one of the highlights of my musical going life."

Sometime later, Dennis, Jared and I would sing that beautiful trio for James Raitt's memorial service after he was taken from us by AIDS in April of 1994, less than two months after we'd opened. Then years later I would sing "Near to You" as a solo this time, for Dennis' memorial in April of 2016 in Chicago. James and Dennis left us much too soon.

Back in San Diego on our first day of rehearsal, we were introduced to our stars—Victor Garber and Bebe Neuwirth. It was exciting. Victor Garber is a wonderful actor, and one of the kindest people I've met in showbiz. Bebe is a triple threat, and a Bob Fosse dancer who understands his movement in her bones. How perfect that she was stepping into the role originally choreographed by Fosse for his wife Gwen Verdon. Bebe had just come off playing the lead in KISS OF THE SPIDERWOMAN in London. But dancer extraordinaire that she is, she is probably best known as Lilith, Frasier's uptight wife on the TV show Cheers. That's the power of the screen.

Finally, on that first day Jack O'Brien called us together. We went through the usual Equity meeting to take care of union business. Then after introductions around the table, Jack began rehearsal with our first readthrough of his adaptation of the original 1950's script. It was exciting to hear the voices of the actors we'd be working with. And though we couldn't know it then, these were the actors we'd be spending the next year of our lives with.

After the readthrough, Jack began blocking the two-person scenes in the main rehearsal room. James Raitt began music rehearsals in another room. And choreography got under way in yet another room with Rob Marshall and his sister Kathleen. Rob is a multi-award-winning theatre choreographer and has since become more widely known as a film director/choreographer and Academy Award winner for directing the film of CHICAGO. Kathleen is also a multi-award-winning choreographer/director, and was for several years artistic director of ENCORES at City Center in New York. So, here we were with rehearsals happening in three spaces at once, while our several producers moved from room to room watching the early process of bringing a show to life. We'd hit the ground running. I was exhilarated and already exhausted. I knew I was part of something much bigger than I'd ever experienced.

We rehearsed for about a month before running our show from October through mid-November. With a brand-new show, especially a brand new updated old-fashioned Broadway musical, that wasn't a lot of time. We did get rewrites on a fairly regular basis, but they were minor as I remember. We had to shut the production down during performance for a day or two, because the set wasn't moving properly. When it was fixed, we went back into performance. There were still some set issues on occasion but not enough to stop the show. And the difficulties didn't dampen the enthusiasm of the Old Globe's opening night audience. We opened to favorable reviews, and audiences loved the production. Our producers were very happy.

San Diego is close enough to LA that all manner of show biz luminaries came to see the show—producers, casting people, actors, writers, directors. And among those who came were the writers of the TV show *Frasier,* who were also the writers of Cheers. They'd come to see Bebe do her thing as Lola, a far cry from Frasier's wife, Lilith.

A week after they'd come to see the show, I got a call from my agent saying that the producers of *Frasier* had a role for me and would I come for a meeting. So, they flew me to LA on a day off, but the casting director Jeff Greenberg was disappointed. "You're so young!" he said. They wanted me to play Martin's girlfriend. Martin is Frasier's father, the role played by John Mahoney. I suppose the 1950's style of dress and hair I was wearing as the long-suffering wife in our show made me seem ten years older. I wanted to say to him, "That's why they call it acting!" But of course, I didn't. He sent me back to San Diego with apologies.

Several days later, my agent called again and said "They want you!" I don't know what had changed their minds. Maybe it had something to do with John Mahoney being a Steppenwolf company member, and my time at Steppenwolf in Chicago. Maybe they simply couldn't find anyone else who seemed right in the time they had. But whatever the reason, they gave me my first job in television. The timing was perfect. We closed DAMN YANKEES on November 14th. *Frasier* filmed the first couple of weeks in December. I would go into rehearsal for the Broadway leg of DAMN YANKEES in January.

A few days after DAMN YANKEES closed, the producers of *Frasier* arranged for a limo to bring Katy dog, Charlie cat and me to our temporary home in The Beverly Hills Sofitel. I had some time to rest before we'd begin work for the two weeks it would take to rehearse and film episode number thirteen of *Frasier*. This was truly surreal.

there is no backstage

W hat I remember of the suite at The Beverly Hills Sofitel is that it was large and plush and very red—red walls, red carpet, red furniture. Charlie nestled into the pillows of the overstuffed big chair and pretty much stayed there for two weeks. I felt pampered staying in this classy hotel, walking my classy little West Highland White Terrier down the streets of Beverly Hills. I felt privileged. I *was* privileged.

Rehearsal began the day after I arrived in LA. That morning, and every morning for the next two weeks, a limo would be waiting outside the Sofitel to take me to Paramount Studios. The first day of rehearsal, I was ushered to a conference room inside the studio where we would do the table read. Sitting around a long table were the cast of *Frasier*—Kelsey Grammer, Jane Leeves, David Hyde- Pierce, Peri Gilpin and John Mahoney as well as the writer/creators David Angell, Peter Casey and David Lee, and a few other actors playing smaller roles. The writer of this particular episode, Molly Newman was also there, as was the episode's director, Andy Ackerman.

There were brief introductions, and then almost immediately, the director began the read through of the episode called "Guess Who's Coming to Breakfast?" The gist of the story is that my character Elaine, a buyer for The Bon Marché lives in the same condo high-rise as Frasier and Martin. Martin and Elaine meet in the hallways of the building one day and he invites her to dinner. After several dates, Martin asks Elaine to his apartment on a night when Frasier is out, and the two of them fall into bed together. Next morning, Elaine wanders into the kitchen to say goodbye to Martin where she unexpectedly meets Frasier. An awkward and very funny breakfast scene follows. Hence, the episode's title. In a little over half an hour the table read was finished, and there was an odd quiet in the room that I didn't understand. After conferring with the writers, Andy said to us, "All right, we'll see you all back here tomorrow."

I remember asking the production manager if that was all for the day and he said, "We'll get you to costumes." So, I was ushered to the costume department where the costume supervisor tried several outfits on me, and the designer, Audrey M. Bansmer decided on the two I'd be wearing. An hour and a half later, I was ushered to the limo and taken back to the Sofitel. It was around noon. Wow. Working in TV seemed so much easier than theatre. Being back so early in the day gave me more than enough time to memorize my lines, so I did. The rest of the day I relaxed. I took Katy for walks. I ordered room service. Then at 11:00 p.m. when I was already in bed, a manila envelope appeared under my hotel room door. It contained changes to the script, but these were not simple changes. This was an almost entirely new script. Wow. Near midnight I had a new scene with new lines to learn. TV was not so easy as I'd thought.

Early the next morning, the limo was waiting to drive me again to Paramount. I was ushered back to the conference room where we did a second table read. When we finished, the writers and director had a private conversation. Then the head writer David Angell said something to the effect of "OK. I think we can work with this one." The pall in the room after the read-through the day before had been the awareness by everyone at the table except me, that the script wasn't up to their standards. It was unusable. I found out much later that they almost scrapped the story entirely and along with it my character and my job. I'm glad I didn't know that. But, for now, they'd keep this latest version to see how it would play.

After a lunch break, we started blocking on Sound Stage twenty-five, or rather the series regulars did. I wasn't in the first scene. I waited in the guest dressing room. My costumes were hanging there. There was a land phone, a couch and a makeup table. But I couldn't sit still, so I went back to the sound stage to watch the process. I was told to wait behind the cameras while they were setting up shots. As I watched Andy block the scenes, I observed how casually these actors took their blocking, said their lines half-energy, learned the shape of the scene given by the director.

David Hyde-Pierce who played Niles had sort of taken me under his wing because I'm sure he could tell how green I was. He is such a generous man. On our break he'd shown me to the canteen, and bought my lunch. Now as we watched rehearsal, I was curious about why the actors were walking onto the set from the camera area, and not from backstage. I assumed it was because this was just the blocking rehearsal, so I asked David how we got to the backstage area. And he answered without any hint of condescension, "There is no backstage."

Oh, my god. I felt like a fool and I was now more nervous than ever. I was having trouble processing what he'd told me. I always stood backstage before a performance, centering myself, disappearing into my character so that she could enter stage for me. How could I disappear with no backstage? I couldn't. So, when rehearsal for my scene was called, I had no choice but to gather my fear and take it with me on set. Then something unexpected happened. I had a visceral realization. I didn't need to disappear. I needed only to show up. And the fear I brought with me fueled my performance. It was a life lesson. It was a lesson in being fully present.

The next day we actors gathered in Kelsey's dressing room just before shooting, to run his last-minute revisions while he got into makeup. And even though I know the cast could see how naïve I was about TV acting—because of course, there is no backstage—they all treated me as if I was one of them. For the three days of shooting, I felt like I was a member of this company of fine actors. And I was. And it was great.

The day after shooting, my animals and I were again carried by limo to the airport where we all flew to Atlanta to pick up my car from my mother's house. We'd leave Charlie cat with Mama, till he could be flown later to New York. My first few months living in New York, I'd be staying in a sublet at 108th and Broadway sharing the condo of a Broadway dancer, who would allow my dog, but not my cat. For now, Katy and I would drive to Chicago to pick up a few things from my condo. Then we'd drive to New York, stopping along the way at my sister and brother-in-law's home in Ohio. It happened to be the night when my *Frasier* episode aired. So, we watched it together. I was very nervous seeing it for the first time with my family, watching before I knew how I'd done. When the episode was finished, I was relieved. My sister was quietly proud, I think. And Mark gave the final approval with "Pretty good." And, it was. It was all pretty good.

CHAPTER NINE

broadway

"Whatever it is you've lost may someday once again be found."

Meg Boyd, DAMN YANKEES

I drove across the George Washington Bridge to the Isle of Manhattan in January of 1994, found my way to 108th Street, and with remarkable ease, I found a parking place on the block where I'd be living. I didn't know for how long. That would depend on whether DAMN YANKEES would succeed on Broadway or be shut down by the critics.

My roommate-to-be owned a condo in a building on 108th near Broadway. I parked my father's little Ford Escort hatchback that Mama had insisted I take, in place of my older Toyota. I'd loved that old boxy-shaped metallic blue Toyota. But the smaller dark grey Escort was newer, and would be a better city car than the Toyota, because in New York I'd have to repark almost daily. Alternate side-of-the-street parking was in place, so the street sweepers could do their job. I certainly didn't want to find myself with a $100+ parking ticket, so trading the Toyota for the Escort was a smart move.

My landlady for a time was a dancer named Camille Degannon. Our choreographer Rob Marshall had given me her number when he heard I was looking for a sublet. She was a beautiful Broadway dancer who'd been working in New York for years. Camille was what we used to call a "gypsy" which is no longer politically correct. But Broadway singer/dancers are certainly travelers who move frequently from show to show. Broadway dancers work more than most leads. Actor/singer/dancers—triple threats, we call them, are always needed. The rest of us are more easily replaced, unless of course the actor has become "the flavor of the month." If she's lucky enough to sit in that position for a while, it's great. But it doesn't last forever. She might be in favor for a show or two, but then "the crown" is inevitably placed on someone else's head. But the really good Broadway triple threat can nearly always find a job.

There is a Broadway dictum that after you've won a Tony, you won't work on a Broadway stage again for five years. That seems to be accurate. But the dancers can usually find another show once theirs has closed, within months. And because of the amount of work they do, dancers are more likely able to create "real lives," to buy homes, marry and have kids. Camille owned her New York apartment. I would never own in the city.

I rested for a couple of days, unpacked my belongings in the one room I'd been given—Camille's second bedroom. The room held one standing cupboard, a futon mattress on the floor, a table and chair, and that was it. But there was light from three huge windows facing South. Together Camille and I created a schedule for sharing the bathroom and kitchen, then I explored our busy neighborhood. I found the best streets for walking my Katy, found the drug store, the grocery store, the closest subway station, and now I was ready to go to work.

Rehearsals began on a Tuesday, downtown Manhattan in the

studios at 890 Broadway, once the Michael Bennett studios. It is a wonderful old building with lots of rehearsal rooms, and ours had a bank of windows across one side opposite mirrors across the other, and the fabulous old wood floor worn from years of dancers' feet. This room carried the magic of all the Broadway shows rehearsed there over the years.

There was a wrench in the works of our early rehearsals, though. We had lost our young Joe Hardy. In the month between our pre-Broadway production in San Diego and rehearsals in New York, Jere Shea had left the show. He had been cast as the lead in the upcoming Broadway production of PASSION by Stephen Sondheim, opening in May just two months after DAMN YANKEES would open in March. Our producers were not happy. It can't have been an easy decision for Jere, but he was in his rights. He'd given proper notice, and creating a lead role in a new Stephen Sondheim musical would be more prestigious. So, that first day of rehearsal we worked on our opening number while Jay Binder's casting agency arranged for auditions to search for our new Joe Hardy.

I took a chance and asked if I could be in on the auditions. Jere and I had established a comfortable, caring rapport, and I worried that finding that rapport with another young man might be tricky. It's not easy for an audience to accept that a beautiful young man might be in love with an older woman, even though the young man is actually the old man inside a young body. The situation needed to play true. I'd made a bold request. Casting was none of my business. I was an actor. Casting was the producers' decision. But since the central love story is between Joe and Meg, I wanted to make sure whoever the new young man was would be as convincing as Jere had been. I wanted to make sure we had chemistry. Jack and Rob agreed to let me be in the audition room.

I read and sang with several young actors auditioning for the part. Finally, the role went to Jarrod Emick who certainly made my job easier, because he played with me as if I was twenty years younger and with a genuine sweetness. I'll never forget something he said in the audition. At one point, Jack told Jarrod that he seemed so comfortable. And Jarrod said, "Oh, I'm scared to death." Jarrod, who'd already played the lead on Broadway as Chris in MISS SAIGON, admitted that he was scared in his audition.

But then, we all are whenever we stand in front of people. An audience may or may not see it, but we all carry some level of anxiety onstage, and certainly in auditions. It only makes sense. We are asking to be hired. And on Broadway, we're asking to be hired for a job that could change our lives and fill our coffers for some time to come.

So, what you do with your nervousness is important. I think Jarrod did the best thing he could have. He recognized it. He even recognized it publicly by telling us. The result was that his nervousness didn't get in his way. It was still there, but it wasn't in the driver's seat. It's the same lesson I'd learned not a month before, rehearsing my episode of *Frasier*, where there was no backstage for me to "disappear." Recognize your fear. Carry it with you. Let it work for you.

I remembered my own audition for DAMN YANKEES, when I was living in Washington Heights after WINGS had closed and before my father died. When I was given the audition, I rented a video of the 1958 film. After I watched it, I thought, "Oh, there's no way I can play this role. She's too much a doormat. I can't have this role be my Broadway debut." But, Jack O'Brien's script reimagined Meg, and I knew she was a character I could live inside. She was no longer the unhappy dishrag of a wife, but the emotional center of the story.

I'd be returning to my roots with this role, to my beginnings in musical theatre. There was something sweet and naïve about this middle-aged character. She carried a girl's romantic longing. So, I decided to audition for her as if Meg was any one of the ingenues I'd played in my twenties. I'd audition for her as a young lover. I like to call Meg Boyd my final ingenue.

The afternoon of my audition, waiting in the hallway at one of the many rehearsal studios in Midtown Manhattan, I was as calm as I'd ever been in my life. I somehow knew the role was mine. I don't know why. When I walked into the room, there must have been twenty or more people behind the auditor's table—director, choreographer, music director, Jay Binder the casting director, Mitchell Maxwell, lead producer, along with a slew of other producers, and all their assistants.

Jack, casual and welcoming as he always was, asked me, "What are you going to sing for us?" I said, "I thought I'd sing 'Simple Little Things' from 110 IN THE SHADE." And after I sang, Jack said "Thank you. That was lovely. Will you read a scene for us?" There were two readers in the room. So, I asked "Who's going to read with me?" Jack said, "Whichever you'd like." I said, "Why not, both. It's a three-person scene." So, I placed the two readers on either side of the room, stood between them, and played the scene. Then Jack asked if I'd sing Meg and young Joe's duet, which I did. Then Jack said, "That was wonderful." And, before he could say, "Thank you, we'll be in touch." I asked him, "Would you like me to sing another song for you? Why don't I?" Jack said, "Why not!" So, I gave the pianist the music to "Is It Really Me?" from 110 IN THE SHADE, and sang. I don't know where the chutzpah came from, but it seemed as though I could do no wrong. I was directing my own audition, and

Jack O'Brien was allowing me to do so. It was the best audition I've ever given.

I walked out of the studio knowing the role was mine. I found out later that half the people in the room wanted to cast me on the spot. But what I didn't know was that the role had already been offered to the wonderful actress, Deborah Monk. She'd been nominated for a Tony for playing the lead in Lanford Wilson's play, REDWOOD CURTAIN, and I was later told that she'd been waiting to accept or refuse the role of Meg, depending on whether she won the Tony. If she won, she'd let the offer for DAMN YANKEES go. I'm grateful I was unaware of that so I could live in the belief that the role was mine. A few days later my happiness would be ripped out of me, on that morning when I was told my father had unexpectedly died. But his passing wasn't truly unexpected. He'd known he had an aortal aneurism that was growing larger, but he hadn't told my sister and me. For us, it was shocking.

I remember the last time I saw my father, standing outside the Zeckendorf Towers in Union Square, where The Public Theatre had housed me for the run of WINGS. The morning after my family had seen the performance, we were waiting for the airport shuttle to arrive, and it was running late. Daddy and I were arguing. He was fretting. He was afraid that he and Mama would miss their flight back to Atlanta. He was being unreasonable. Shuttles always allow for more time than needed to get their passengers to the airport. But Daddy was agitated in a way I didn't understand. He wasn't himself, and I was impatient with him. I don't remember now what I said, but I do remember his eyes. He was angry, but I saw something more in him. Now I believe that what I saw must've been fear. Of dying maybe, before he could get home to Atlanta. And sorrow maybe, for not being able to tell me he was dying, knowing that this would likely be the last time we'd see one another. I think he was close to telling me his secret when the shuttle arrived. Years later, my mother told me she felt that seeing WINGS, watching Emily's courageous flight toward the unknown had helped my father with his own passing. I hope that was true. As I watched him board the shuttle that morning, I could not know that in less than a month my life would change twice. First by the call telling me of my father's death, and second by the call I received the day before his funeral telling me I was cast in my first Broadway show. That was June of 1993.

Now in January of 1994, Jarrod Emick was cast in his second Broadway lead and he joined our rehearsals. Three weeks later we moved from the rehearsal studio to the theatre at The Marriott Marquis on forty-sixth and Broadway. We were going into tech rehearsals for the few weeks it would take to be ready for an audience. It's impossible to forget our first audience, the invited dress rehearsal, what we then called the "gypsy run-through." It was a full house. It felt like half the actors in New York showed up for the free first performance. And we played to that full house of theatre people laughing at every joke, cheering every musical number. There is nothing like playing to an audience of theatre people in a big Broadway house. It remains the most enthusiastic, the most joyful audience I've experienced in my fifty years of performing. It was wonderful!

And so, we were open. To fantastic reviews. "DAMN YANKEES hits a home run!" Clive Barnes of the *New York Post*. "A Stunning, Heartening Revival", John Simon with *New York Magazine*. Oh my god. I got my own from William A. Henry III of *Time Magazine,* "Linda Stephens makes a stunning Broadway debut!" Wow. The show was working. The show was selling. And that meant we'd run for at least six months. And so now it was time for me to move to a more permanent place.

I found a beautiful little studio apartment, a condo sublet in Brooklyn Heights. It was the first stop from Manhattan under the East River on the #2 subway. The apartment was such a short train ride from Times Square, that it was almost like living in Manhattan. The apartment was on the top floor of a six-floor building, in the southwest corner which meant I'd have beautiful sunsets, because also, the apartment was banked with casement windows. It had been beautifully renovated, painted a light mauve, with a yellow-tiled bathroom that also had a window. There was a window in the galley-style kitchen as well. There was a pass-through from the kitchen to the main large living area. And for $900 a month, which now would be nearly three times that, I rented this little condo.

The owner had built floor to ceiling shelves on the wall opposite the windows. There was an entrance hall with two large closets behind both hallway walls, which gave an L-shape to the apartment. The hallway was large enough for someone to bunk on the foldout ottoman I'd bought from Castro Convertibles to go with the convertible sleeper couch I'd bought for the main room. The small table and chairs I'd bought fit perfectly under the kitchen pass-through. Though it was only a studio there was a sense of space in this little apartment.

I had no kitchenware, no sheets and towels, so my friend Rosie Prinz gave me all her old silverware and a few pots and pans. I bought whatever else I felt I'd need for the next month or so. Castro delivered my couch and ottoman. My friend Jeff Lunden found a truck to help me haul the newly bought table and chairs, and the rest of my things from the apartment on 108th. And we drove down the West Side Highway on the Isle of Manhattan, then under the East River in the Brooklyn-Battery Tunnel to Red Hook, then North to Brooklyn Heights, and unloaded.

Now my Katy and I were home, and it was time for Mama to put Charlie cat on a plane by himself to fly from Atlanta to New York. I picked him up at La Guardia, traumatized but well, and drove him home to Brooklyn.

We needed only one more thing to make the place home, and my friend Michael Russell just happened to be selling his Yamaha Clavinova, so I bought it. Now that we had our piano, our new home was complete. My two animals and I were ready to find out what it meant to be living and working in New York.

To celebrate my first night in the apartment, I stepped out the living room window onto the fire escape landing, glass of Chardonnay in hand, and discovered beneath me the beautifully-kept garden belonging to the First Presbyterian Church that fronted Henry Street around the corner. And in the distance, I watched the sun set behind the Brooklyn skyline and wondered, "How in the world did I get here?"

I've lived in so many different places in my life, but only a few have truly felt like home and this was one of them—this beautiful, open, yellow and mauve studio apartment in the Southwest corner on the sixth floor of 70 Clark Street, Brooklyn Heights.

* * *

We were into an open-ended run, which meant that we'd play as long as the show was making money for the producers. It's a curious occupation, running a show. It is comparable to, but not the same as having a nine to five job. But instead of working in the day, you're working six nights a week, plus two afternoons—eight shows a week. Your "weekend" is one day not two, and usually Monday. It is very much a job. Acting may be your work, but running a show is your job.

Broadway shows have different schedules, and ours was probably the easiest, with a Wednesday matinee which meant we didn't do the brutal five-show weekend—Friday night with two on Saturday and two on Sunday. A Wednesday matinee meant we'd have Sunday night off, and next to the regular Monday off and all-day Tuesday till showtime, it felt almost like a full weekend.

An open-ended run is a strange way to live life for a while. You know the job will end at some point but you don't know when, and the job sculpts the rest of your life, shaping when you eat, sleep, do laundry, see friends and family, do anything outside the show. Your entire life is about reserving energy to be used at the highest level you can muster at the wrong end of the day, the time when the body should be resting. It's unnatural, this business of performing.

The job itself requires giving the same performance eight times a week. You wear the same costumes, say the same words, sing the same melodies, do the same movement. But whenever an actor is interviewed about running a show, you'll often hear her say, "Oh, it's different every night." And that's true. But the differences are subtle, and you begin to drop deeper into the role as your understanding of what you're saying, what your relationships are, what the audience is telling you, begins to expand. Inside yourself, those discoveries seem huge, but on the surface, they are very small. They're about a new sense of meaning, a gesture, an inflection. For the actor, the meaning of the character and the story becomes clearer. An audience might not notice the difference if they saw two performances in a row. But

I believe they'd feel it. And their experience would be richer as the actor's show deepens.

Running DAMN YANKEES, I remember going through periods where I'd experience a series of days when it seemed I couldn't engage in the show and the work became tedious. But then something would shift, and I'd experience a reinvestment in the performance, and was now moving through a time when there were nightly discoveries. I never understood what brought about these shifts. But there was something natural about them, almost like the phases of the moon, or the movement of tides.

There is also what seems to be a natural breakdown of a Broadway show that happens as actors leave and are replaced by others. An actor will leave a show because she's found another job, or sometimes because she just can't do it anymore, or maybe because she's been injured. Replacement actors will always look like the actor who came before, but they may not always have the same skills. I felt that most keenly when Jarrod Emick left our show sometime in early 1995, and we went through a series of Young Joes. They were all beautiful young men, and wonderful singer/dancers, but the rapport Jarrod and I'd built through rehearsal and the long run of performances, couldn't be created in a replacement rehearsal or two. And that's all these young actors got. So, I felt I had to play our scene for both of us. I had to show my love for Young Joe, and somehow show his love for Meg. That's when my show began to disintegrate. My show was about relationship and what I'd feared might happen when Jere left, was happening when Jarrod left. Everything became generalized. That was to show itself most clearly in Meg and Joe's dishwashing scene.

Jack O'Brien had choreographed the dishwashing while the couple sings "A Man Doesn't Know". Every gesture, every cup and every plate was handled specifically to support the words of the song. And, the movement was beautifully subtle. But we'd gone through a series of replacement stage managers as well, and somehow those specifics had never been written down by stage management. So, with each new Young Joe, I had to teach as best I could the dish choreography. But the movement was never again the same, so the meaning behind those movements was gone. The scene lost depth.

Now, nine or ten months into our run, our show began to go through multiple replacements. And on top of that, people got sick, or dancers were injured, or actors went on vacation. So, every performance, we'd check the sign-in board to see who was in the show and who was out. But there was another replacement in our show that would change the production dramatically. Jerry Lewis.

It's remarkable to think that Jerry Lewis had never been in a Broadway show. He told us that his father had always wanted to see his son on Broadway. His father was gone now. But being in a Broadway show was the only thing that would fully legitimize Jerry as performer in his father's eyes. At least, that's what he told us. So, after Jerry saw our show, he was in touch with the producers, and quickly went about the business of offering his services to play The Devil when Victor Garber decided to leave. Jerry not only replaced Victor after we'd run a year, but he became the primary producer when the production went on tour.

We had January of 1995 off after Victor left our show, and then Jerry took over in February. We ran on Broadway another six months before Jerry took the show on tour. My show had been compromised with Jarrod's leaving, and I felt I couldn't play my role as truthfully as I had. So, I chose not to play at all, and the show went on the road without me. But for six months, I got to play with my first movie star crush. My high school dream fella wasn't Rock Hudson or Paul Newman or Robert Redford, it was Jerry Lewis. Truly. He did a movie called CINDERFELLA, a takeoff on the Cinderella fairy tale, and when his fairy godfather transformed his ragged clothes into a handsome red tuxedo so he could dance with the princess at the ball, my young heart flipped.

Maybe it was partly the rags to riches story that moved me, but more than that, I was drawn to his comedy—the silly, sweet, slapstick comedy that he made look so easy. I was in love with the child I saw inside him, that brilliant boychild who could fool everyone into believing he was a prince. I identified with that boychild as the young small-town girl I once was, who could fool everyone into believing she was a princess. And so, odd as it seems, I saw myself in him.

I remember Jerry's put-in rehearsal for DAMN YANKEES. He was wearing the Devil's costumes while the rest of us were in street clothes under work lights. His put-in was just like all the other replacement rehearsals during our run. He wasn't treated specially. He didn't want to be treated differently. So, it wasn't until his first performance that he saw the rest of us in costume under stage light.

I remember Jerry warming up every performance by listening to Frank Sinatra on the huge sound system he'd had brought into his large onstage dressing room. It was the "star" dressing room given to all the leads in shows performing at the Marquis Theatre. And I remember the day Liza Minnelli came to see the show, and after the performance, the stage manager called the entire cast to Jerry's dressing room where Jerry "presented" Liza to us like a proud father.

I remember Jerry making fun, imitating me when I had to power out a note a little below my range in "Near to You." It felt like a stamp of approval being mocked by Jerry Lewis.

I remember Jerry supplying us all with expensive cough drops and mints and chocolates. Jerry would buy out an entire Italian restaurant in downtown Manhattan more than once, for the cast and crew to have dinner after a performance. He was generous and genuinely friendly with the entire cast and crew. He knew us individually. But he was also very much a businessman. Every choice he made seemed to be toward keeping DAMN YANKEES running. I think he wanted to run the show until he died. He almost did.

I remember Jerry sitting in my dressing room before a performance one night asking if I was going to do the tour with him. How strange it felt to be hosting him in my room, telling him that I couldn't do the tour, because I'd lost my show when Jarrod left. I felt I was disappointing him. And if I knew then what I know now, I might have gone on the road with him. It would be five years before I was on Broadway again.

I remember most of all sharing stage with Jerry in the most ridiculous of situations. There is a scene in the play after young Joe has moved back into his home as Meg's boarder. She of course doesn't know that this young man is her husband. But she feels a deep connection with him, and they become friends. The Devil doesn't want Joe to be distracted by his feelings for his wife and wants him to move back in with the other ball players. So, the Devil disguised as Mr. Applegate disguised as The Fire Chief, wearing a big yellow slicker and a yellow plastic fireman's hat, comes to Meg's house and knocks on the door. I, as Meg, open the door to Jerry Lewis disguised as The Devil disguised as Mr. Applegate disguised as The Fire Chief, who then says to me:

"Are you the LAAAAAADY of the house?"

Oh My God. Well. I don't believe there was a performance when the audience didn't fall out laughing. And most of the time, I lost it. Jerry broke too, because he was an easy mark. But there was method in his madness, because he knew that audiences love watching the actor "break" onstage. So, he took the opportunity to do a little ad-libbing. And I never knew what would come out of his mouth, where he would take the riffing, and for how long. It was my job in that moment to be his straight man. Then when it was time to move on, and only he knew when that was, he'd steer the show back into the script. What silliness! What fun! What brilliance! What a privilege to be his Dean Martin, eight shows a week.

For me though, that moment was something more. Not only was I onstage playing with my high school movie star crush, I was being transported in memory to my Harlequin Theatre days. Turns out that all those years before, I had played many a similar moment. I was being trained to play straight man to Jerry Lewis, by another comic master, Larry Shue.

larry like jerry

L arry would leave the stage as Charley's Aunt, soaked through
from skin to black lace. He was playing Charley in WHERE'S
CHARLEY?, having donned the garb of Charley's Aunt, a huge black
floor-length dress trimmed in black lace, and wearing a black mantilla
on top of his steely grey old-lady wig. His intention as character was
to convince his beloved's mother that he was worthy of her hand. His
intention as actor was something wickedly different.

The height of his wickedness came in "the tea scene" when the
entire cast was onstage, when Larry disguised as Charley disguised
as Charley's Aunt was pouring tea for the five of us. He had us and
the audience in the palm of his hand, because his main goal, his only
purpose at that moment was to make us all laugh. And more than
that, to make us fall so uncontrollably into laughter that we actors
would have to turn upstage and hide our faces.

He'd make up little stories, do little dances with the teacups and
saucers, turn them into puppets. He made up a language for them
to speak. Whatever it took, he would mercilessly do just to make us
break character, to make us laugh. And he wasn't happy until all five
of us had given in and turned upstage every performance of the run.
And Larry as Charley as Charley's Aunt always succeeded.

Why? Because he could. It was his brilliance. Because the musical
itself was a comedy, and his antics weren't out of character with the
story. Because Ray Bolger who had originally played the role came up
with his own antics at that point, and the script gives permission for
any actor playing the role to do the same. So, Larry did.

And Larry like Jerry Lewis knew that one of the things an audience loves most is watching an actor breakup on stage. So, Larry kept polishing that out-of-script bit until it shone, until it was complete. Larry never worried about compromising the story because he always knew, like Jerry, just when to guide us back into the play.

Little did we know then that those antics in "the tea scene" in our production of WHERE'S CHARLEY, were the seeds planted that would blossom into a story told in an imaginary language in a play Larry would write years from then, THE FOREIGNER. In his play, there is "the breakfast scene" where Larry gives the actors permission to make up their own imaginary business with cups and plates and forks, speaking in a fake foreign language, with the only object being to stop the show and make people laugh, preferably uncontrollably. There are two characters in the breakfast scene, Ellard who's not very smart, and the foreigner who's smarter than everyone else in the play, and whose name is not surprisingly, Charlie. Different spelling, same spirit. Brilliant!

Larry Shue as Charley, WHERE'S
CHARLEY, Harlequin Atlanta, 1975

Eliza Dolittle,
MY FAIR LADY,
with Larry Shue
as Henry Higgins,
Illinois Wesleyan
University, 1968

Maria, WEST SIDE STORY,
Theatre at Fort Lee, 1970

Singing at the Officers Club,
Fort Lee, VA, 1971

Lizzy Curry,
110 IN THE SHADE
with Jack Kyrieleison,
Harlequin Dinner
Theater, 1975

Talkback for THE NIGHT OF THE IGUANA with Tennessee Williams, Liza Nelson, Fred Chappell and me, The Alliance Theatre, 1980

Hannah Jelkes, THE NIGHT OF THE IGUANA, The Alliance Theatre, 1980

Blanche DuBois, A STREETCAR NAMED DESIRE, The Alliance Theatre, 1983

Gertrude, HAMLET with John Frederick
Jones, Alabama Shakespeare Festival, 1980

Gertrude, HAMLET with Greg Martin,
The Alliance Theatre, 1986

Gertrude, HAMLET with Saxon Palmer, Georgia Shakespeare Festival, 1999

Emily Stilson, WINGS,
Imaginary Theatre, 1979

Emily Stilson, WINGS, Goodman Theatre,
1992

Emily Stilson, WINGS, The Public Theater, 1993

Yelena, UNCLE VANYA,
Alabama Shakespeare
Festival, 1980

Mrs. Gibbs, OUR TOWN with Freda
Norman as Mrs. Webb, Omsk State
Drama Theatre, Siberia, 1992

Linda Loman, DEATH OF A SALESMAN
with Ken Albers, The Milwaukee Rep, 1992

Jerry Lewis, his son, Mama and me, opening night party for DAMN YANKEES at Tavern on the Green, New York City, 1995

Dennis Kelly and me, DAMN YANKEES, New York City, 1994

Terry Beaver and me, THE MAN WHO CAME TO DINNER, New York City, 2000

Art Perlman, Jeff Lunden and Thomas Z. Shepard prepping the recording of WINGS, 1994

Backstage after SUNDAY IN THE PARK WITH GEORGE, with Flo Lacey, Melissa Erico, Barbara Cook and me, Kennedy Center, 2002

Harvey Schmidt in rehearsal, GROVER'S CORNERS, Marriott Lincolnshire Theatre, 1987

Helen Martins,
THE ROAD TO
MECCA with
Bri Sudia, Renaissance
Theaterworks, 2013

Maggie, MEMORY HOUSE with Christina
Panfilio, Renaissance Theatreworks, 2006

Nancy, SEASCAPE with Jim Pickering,
Milwaukee Rep, 2007

Betty Meeks, THE FOREIGNER with Brendan Meyer, Matt Zambrano and
Cristina Panfilio, The Milwaukee Rep, 2016

CHAPTER TEN

the run

"You can open any door. There's nothin' to it but to do it."

The Ball Players, DAMN YANKEES

N ow there was time to relax. I didn't have to worry about income, about where the next month's rent was coming from. I was living in a beautiful historical neighborhood in Brooklyn. I was playing one of the second leads in a popular Broadway musical. There had even been talk of my being nominated for a Tony. But the week before the Tony nominations were announced, GREASE opened. And Marcia Lewis, a beloved actress who'd been in New York for a long time, was given what might have been my nomination. That's what Jim Carnahan, my agent at the time, told me.

There were only four nominations in each category. And for this category, best featured actress in a musical, besides Marcia were Sally Mayes for SHE LOVES ME, Marin Mazzie for PASSION, and in a role that I'd auditioned for around the same time I auditioned for DAMN YANKEES, Audra McDonald for CAROUSEL. Audra won. It was her breakout role, and the first of her now six Tonys. It wouldn't have been mine if I had been nominated. Such a rich group of actresses. But for there to have been scuttlebutt on the street about a nomination for my work in DAMN YANKEES, was unbelievable to me.

So, life was good. I was successful according to society's standards for the first time in my life. I had friends in the city and friends from out of town coming to the city to see the show. And celebrities came to see our show nightly. After the show one night I opened my dressing room door to find Irene Worth and Christopher Walken who'd come to see the play together. Here they were, these two actors I held high, delivering kudos to us all. And to me personally, Christopher Walken said, "Great performance." It didn't seem real. I'd seen these two only on screen. I couldn't even find the words to thank them properly, to tell them how much I loved their work. I was discombobulated.

I had similar experiences with other celebrities who would show up backstage. Another night I left my dressing room for the stage, to make my final entrance. Someone was standing in the wings stage left, watching the show. It was Martin Short. He was watching his friend Victor Garber playing The Devil. They'd known one another since they were young, performing in a now famous Toronto production of GODSPELL, which included Eugene Levy, Gilda Radner and Andrea Martin. Ms. Martin would also show up backstage from time to time. I couldn't process it. I was about to enter stage, leaving Martin Short to watch Dennis and me sing the end of the show with Victor as The Devil screaming "Nooooo!" as he descended into hell, which was of course the trap room below stage. I didn't know what to say to Martin Short, whose work I love. I felt shy and clumsy. So, I said nothing.

I remember standing backstage during the ball players' first big solo number—The Blooper Ballet—amazed by the marriage of athleticism and artistry in our dancing ballplayers. They were thrilling to watch. And there was one night when one of the ball players came down from a leap and hurt his foot. He quickly left stage and was almost immediately replaced by the swing dancer who'd been standing in the wings. It took less than 30 seconds for one dancer to leave stage and the other to enter replacing him. From the house, it was a kind of sleight of hand. Or in this case, maybe a sleight of foot. The audience never knew that one ball player had been replaced by another in the middle of a wild dance number. It was magic. And watching from backstage it took my breath away.

I remember our second opening night, this one for Jerry's 1995 stint as The Devil. I'd not allowed my mother to come for the first opening. I knew it would be too much for me to give Mama attention while I'd be going through the biggest opening of my life with its parties and interviews and unknowns. But for Jerry's opening, Mama was there. We were sitting at a table at the opening night party at Tavern on the Green in Central Park. I got up quickly to get us another piece of cake and accidentally bumped into the older gentleman behind me, and when I apologized, he congratulated me on my performance and introduced himself as Douglas Fairbanks, Jr. Oh, my God. How was it possible that I was able to introduce my mother to Robin Hood's son? And of course, I introduced her to Jerry, whom I caught on the fly working the party. I have a wonderful photo of that introduction. Jerry is shaking Mama's hand, with me between them making the introduction, and Jerry's son who was his bodyguard, is standing behind him.

I remember going out the stage door nightly, being greeted by audience members waiting for autographs, and not just for Jerry's. New York theatre fans are intense. There was one man who'd created a book of clippings of my work, and besides DAMN YANKEES he had clippings from WINGS in both New York and Chicago, and he had even earlier press going back to my college days. I was flattered but a little unsettled. I mean who does that? How did he find all that about my early days? And why? That was a small taste of what it must feel like to be a big celebrity.

Still, to be treated as a star is ego-pumping. Even when you like to believe your ego doesn't need stroking, you feel it rise like a puppy to be petted by whoever offers praise. I remember going through a time during the run of the show, watching myself get a little too used to the overabundance of nightly praise. I began to understand why, when actors rise in celebrity, old friends sometimes fall away, as new more prominent friends take their place. I felt those tendencies rising in me. And I thought, "No, I won't go down that road." And I didn't. But honestly, I never rose quite high enough on the showbiz ladder to truly know how much I might be changed. I got used to the praise waiting for me at the stage door. I got used to the celebrities coming backstage to congratulate me. I began to expect it. But I also began to arm myself against it, because the only energy I had after the show was for battling people on the street in Times Square to make my way down the subway, to go home and have a drink.

Go home and have a drink, or two, or three. I remember the bar on the first floor of my apartment building in Brooklyn Heights. It seemed incongruous to the neighborhood. But it was a holdover from earlier days before the neighborhood began to gentrify. It was a seedy old bar. Smoky, with pool tables, dart boards, dark wood furniture—a neighborhood bar. But the customers frequenting this bar lived in other, rougher Brooklyn neighborhoods, having been booted out by the rising cost of living in Brooklyn Heights. Still, these folks hung onto "their" bar.

Most of the time I'd come home from the show, walk my Katy,

then open a bottle of wine, sit in front of the TV and wind down. But there were times when loneliness took over, and the bar in the bowels of my building pulled at me. So, I'd follow that need to connect with someone, with anyone. I remember one night, sitting at the bar next to a young man named Billy, having a drunken conversation about who knows what, agreeing with one another, no matter what came out of our mouths. We were like the "two lost souls" in the duet the Devil and Lola sing to one another in the show. We were both so drunk that when he asked me to go home with him, I did. I didn't even think about it. I just went with him. We walked to his place which seemed miles away, then up flights of stairs. I wanted to keep talking. I wanted the company. He did too. But he wanted it in another way. So, I gave him what he wanted, and stayed with him. I stayed the night.

Dawn, the next morning, I walked down to the street and had no idea where I was. I walked in the direction I thought we'd come from the night before. I recognized nothing. Three quarters of an hour later, I found my building. I walked my dog.

What I'd done was stupid. It was dangerous. And even moreso, it was sad. I knew that. I knew if I hadn't had so much to drink, I'd never have gone home with him. I knew I was in the bar in the first place because even though my life was rich with blessings, I was deeply unhappy. I knew it was time to find another therapist. So, I did. Her name was Rachel, and she helped me begin looking at myself more clearly. Third session with her, Rachel asked me why I'd really come to see her. I told her I didn't know why I was so lonely. And she said to me "I think you've come here to stop drinking." So, I did. Three months into the run of DAMN YANKEES, I stopped drinking.

life after broadway

"I can't think about this now. I'll think about it tomorrow."

Scarlett O'Hara, GONE WITH THE WIND

D AMN YANKEES closed on Broadway, August sixth, 1995. After the performance came down that evening, there were tears and hugs and goodbyes. We packed up our dressing rooms and met in the lobby where the producers were delivering speeches of thanks and offering champagne toasts. It'd been a year and three months since I'd had anything to drink, but with the close of this longest run of my life, this huge job that had given me so much and had demanded all I that had to offer for a year and a half, I took the glass of champagne and toasted with my company of players. It seemed right, and it was good. Then after the producers' toast, I celebrated for hours with my stage husband Dennis Kelly, his wife Ami and a few others. Then I did the same thing I'd done for the last year and a half, six nights a week. I battled the crowd in Times Square, went down the subway, took the #2 train to Brooklyn Heights, and this important passage in my life was over.

So, I gave myself time to recover from the events of the last two years. I'd been living inside Meg Boyd first in San Diego and then

New York. Before that I'd been living inside Emily Stilson in WINGS in Chicago and then New York. And between those two life-changing productions in my life, I had moved from Chicago to New York. Most affecting of all, my father had died. I was reeling from all the movement in my life, and I needed to stop, to rest.

After only a few weeks, I fell back into the pattern of the out-of-work New York actor. Taking auditions, arranging coffees and lunches with friends, walking the Brooklyn Bridge for exercise. I did a couple of TV episodes for the now closed New York Undercover. And in a Spin City episode I played Michael J. Fox's prospective mother-in-law. That was another surreal experience, playing with the man who up until then I'd only seen on screen. And I was still clumsy around stars. There was one point during a break in shooting when Michael J. Fox looked at me and said, "What's wrong with you?" I was having trouble making chit chat on breaks while the camera crews reset. I was nearly frozen. What was wrong with me was that I felt I wasn't good enough to be there. I couldn't enjoy the experience. I forgot that all I needed to do was show up, be fully present. I learn my life lessons slowly. I could act with Michael J. Fox, but I didn't know how to be with him.

During this time after Broadway, I was also recording books. Recorded Books, Incorporated had hired me to record a young adult book called *Sing Down the Moon,* as a test, and I had passed. That was the first month of my run of DAMN YANKEES, and for the next twenty-five years, Recorded Books continued to give me work, even after I'd moved away from New York. The most prestigious book I recorded was *Gone with the Wind.* It's an exclusive recording because the Margaret Mitchell estate wanted the book recorded in its entirety, and Recorded Books is the only company that agreed to do the unabridged version. They gave me the job of narrator.

This was one of the few times when Recorded Books auditioned their narrators. I won the audition because of the way I narrated the black voices in the story. Margaret Mitchell had written out a dialect for the black characters, but it was very thick, almost cartoonish, and frankly, hard to follow. So, the dialect needed adapting for the narration. Mine I suppose, was the most subtle of the interpretations. I tried to speak from the heart of the characters. But these characters were written by a white woman in 1936, and so it wasn't only the dialects that were skewed, it was the black characters themselves. They were there to serve their masters most often in kind-hearted ways. They served functions in Margaret Mitchell's story. The book is a fiction, and it was born out of an era before America had begun to scratch the surface of systemic racism that runs through our society. But, it's an important book. It holds the mirror up to our country's nature.

It took ninety-six hours to record *Gone with the Wind.* The finished recording is forty-nine hours. I was nominated for an AUDI, the "Tony" for recorded books. The nomination was for best narration of a classic book, but I lost to Kate Burton for her narration of *A Tree Grows in Brooklyn.* Kate's voice resonates her father, Richard Burton's beautifully rich voice. I'd played Kate's sister in a Brien Friel play called THE ARISTOCRATS years before at The Huntington Theatre in Boston. Our paths had never crossed again until the AUDI ceremony, and our paths have never crossed since. That's show biz.

It was because of *Gone with the Wind* that I became one of the go-to Southern female voices at Recorded Books, Inc. And my favorite Southern author to narrate is Lee Smith. I've recorded quite a few of her books, among them her wonderful *The Last Girls,* for which I was given a Golden Earphones Award from Audiophile. Lee's stories are colorful, rich, authentic. And the soul of her writing resonates with me. I've loved giving voice to her characters.

Because New York was still giving me work, I decided to drive back to Chicago, find a real estate agent and put my little condo on the market. I found a company to sell my furniture including the wonderful old farmer's table I've long wished I had kept, and my piano, an old Kimball studio upright. It fell out of tune so quickly that I'd learned how to tune it myself. It seems that if you can tune a violin, you can tune a piano, just takes a little longer. Tuning that old piano had become a form of meditation. I've missed getting lost in its resonances, for the couple of hours it took to tune the Kimball.

I'd brought Katy with me on the trip. Charlie was in the New York apartment being fed daily by my downstairs neighbor on Clark Street who was also an actress. We'd help one another out from time to time, picking up mail, feeding animals. She'd climb out her fire-escape window, and up the stairs to my apartment, to keep Charlie company for a while. While I was in Chicago, I drove to Glen Ellyn, Illinois, and stayed for a few days with Dolores and Percy, Larry's parents. They would remain in my life until they passed away several years later. They were like second parents to me. I miss them both in the world.

My own mother had come to visit me in New York for Christmas in both 1994 and 1995. We'd see the Rockettes at Radio City, and Prairie Home Companion live onstage at Town Hall. Christmas in New York is spectacular. There is so much to do. We'd watch the skaters on the rink below the huge Christmas tree at Rockefeller Center with the smell of roasted chestnuts in the air. Mama and I shared Hanukkah with my friend Jeff and his brother Glenn and Glenn's partner Frank, along with their childhood friend Lee, who always made the latkes to go with Glenn's brisket. Jeff would also take Mama and me to The Big Apple Circus set up behind Lincoln Center. I think Mama had fun. It was sometimes hard to tell. The experience was so far away from any traditional Christmas celebration. Christmas in New York may have seemed bizarre for Mama. I felt responsible for giving her as much of the New York experience as I could. She seemed to enjoy herself, but she sometimes seemed to drop into herself. I don't know if she felt insecure in these different situations, or felt she needed to "put on a show" to find a way to present herself. Mama was always good at "putting on a show," the job of a salesman's wife. But of course, the salesman was gone now. Maybe that was part of the remove I felt from her. Twenty-five years later when she was in memory care, eight hours away from my home, I wondered still who was behind that "show." Even on her 98th birthday she put up a kind of facade when I visited. I had a deep connection with my mother, a bond that was formed during the first seven years of my life when Daddy was on the road for days at a time, and my sister was not yet born. But still, I don't think I ever truly knew my Mama. I'm not sure anybody did.

CHAPTER TWELVE

steppenwolf to williamstown

"What more can we be?"

Kate Keller, ALL MY SONS

In the winter of 1996, I was asked to meet with Max Mayer, who was directing a new play at Steppenwolf called, SUPPLE IN COMBAT by Alexandra l. Gersten-Vassilaros. We met in a studio in Manhattan, and the first thing he said to me was, "You're so young!" They wanted me to play Martha Lavey's mother. Martha was eleven years younger than me. Max was remembering me in WINGS, in makeup and wig, playing a woman in her early eighties. Like the time in the *Frasier* casting office, I wanted to say, "That's why they call it acting!" But since he knew I could play older and had won all those awards in Chicago and New York playing older, he cast me. I drove to Chicago in early February where Charlie and Katy and I were put up in actor housing, a couple of blocks from the theatre.

Martha Lavey was a brilliant woman. Actress, director, and artistic director of Steppenwolf Theatre Company from 1995-2015 when she passed away too early at age sixty. In this 1996 production she was playing John Mahoney's wife. I'd of course already worked with John in *Frasier* three years earlier. Then I was playing his girlfriend who they'd initially thought I was too young for, and now I was playing his mother-in-law. What's wrong with this picture? This wouldn't be the last time I'd be cast as mother to an actor only a few years younger than me. A few years later, I'd play Mrs. Higgins to a Henry who was four years my junior. But it isn't my experience only of being cast much older than I am. All actresses somewhere between their mid-40's and early 50's are thrown into competition with actresses in their 60's and 70's. That's not an exaggeration. We're lumped into one group—The Older Actress. Jim Carnahan, my one-time agent, once told me that I'd reached an age where I was "one of them." So, at a certain age, we actresses are no longer thought of as individuals but as "one of them." There may be exceptions, but becoming "one of them" is the inevitable, unwelcome rite of passage for the older actress. Older actors have a similar passage, but theirs is not quite so limiting as ours. That's my observation.

Of course, you can choose the roles you say yes to, based on a list of personal requirements. One of the requirements on my list is whether or not I need the money. In this case, I did need the money. Also, I'd been offered this role without audition, which was generous. So, I said yes to the job. Besides, I'd be playing at Steppenwolf. Who doesn't want to work at Steppenwolf with two such exceptional artists as John Mahoney and Martha Lavey. They're both gone now. And the theatre is less rich without them.

When I accepted the work, I hadn't said yes to the role. I'd said yes to the job. And, it's important when saying yes to know the difference. Sometimes it's OK to say yes to the money. But if the role doesn't speak to you in any real way, then it might be best to say no if you're at all able. This was the first time I remember struggling deeply with a character. I struggled with playing this older character who was an alcoholic. Maybe it was too close for comfort. She was an alcoholic who was not only unhappy, but an inept mother. She wasn't caring, she was self-absorbed. I couldn't find my way into her. I guess I didn't want to find my way into her. I didn't want to find my way back into my own alcoholism to use as fodder for the character. I kept asking for us to rehearse and break down moments, but I didn't realize that what was I truly asking was to make the character more sympathetic than she actually was. I thought the character was one-dimensional, and I just didn't like her. The way my body dealt with it was to get very sick.

I caught an upper-respiratory virus, and couldn't go to rehearsal for several days. Max came to my apartment to talk to me. He asked me if I wanted to leave the production. They'd understand because they knew it wasn't working for me. It wasn't working for them either. I was holding up rehearsals. I'd never been irresponsible, but now it seemed I was. I told him that I couldn't justify leaving the play. I went back to rehearsal the next day. But, when we got to tech rehearsals, Max was at the end of his tether with me and said, "Just do the scene as fast as you can." So, I did. He told me, "That's it. That's good. Keep that!" I felt that all I was doing was singing and dancing the role, playing nothing but rhythm. But it was effective. When we performed the play and my character left stage after her one scene, there was applause...mid-act applause. It hearkened back to my playing Birdie in THE LITTLE FOXES at the Alliance Theatre, leaving stage after a monologue to mid-act applause. Birdie was an alcoholic too. I must play them well. That's unsettling.

The show had opened on May eighth and was to run through June thirtieth. During the early part of the run, I got a call from Jay Binder Casting in New York. They wanted me to play the mother in the Fiftieth Anniversary production of Arthur Miller's ALL MY SONS at The Williamstown Theatre Festival in Massachusetts. Rehearsals would begin overlapping the last two weeks of my run at Steppenwolf. I went to Martha and asked if they'd release me from my contract to do the job at Williamstown. She wasn't happy. I couldn't blame her. I'd been a problem for this production from the beginning. But she let me out of the contract. My understudy would play the last two weeks of the run. That was more than generous. I said thank you, with many apologies. The Jeff Award Committee would later nominate me for my performance. It was the only cameo nomination that year, so I was given the award. I couldn't be there to receive it. Ironic.

I did my last performance of SUPPLE IN COMBAT on Saturday June fifteenth, and after six hours of sleep, I got in my Daddy's little Ford Escort, animals in tow, and drove ten hours toward Williamstown, Massachusetts. The timing belt on the car broke just inside New York State, conveniently at a toll booth. It was towed to a little town called Ripley, a lazy little town, and I spent Sunday night in The Colonial Squires Motel, sitting alongside a grape orchard. Monday morning, Swan's garage fixed the car, and at 1:00 p.m. I left for Williamstown. Rehearsal began on Tuesday.

* * *

At Williamstown, the company management had lost my housing. They thought they'd found a place that would take pets, but they'd been misinformed. And so, my animals and I were taken to a motel while management looked for pet-friendly housing. The Tuesday morning that rehearsal began, eighty-one-year-old Arthur Miller walked into the room and said, "Hello." There were introductions, handshakes, and he said to us, "Well you all look like the parts you're playing." We did. Then Mr. Miller left us to get on with our first read-through. It was a very good cast. Broadway's most recent Billy Bigelow, Michael Hayden was playing Chris, and Joe Costa was playing Joe. Angie Phillips, Stephen Turner, Kate Hampton, Stephanie Mnookin, Kevin O'Rourke, Liam Craig, and Henry Smith were the rest. Our director was thirty-one-year-old Rhodes Scholar, Barry Edelstein who reminded me so much of my second husband Kent, with his quick intelligence, his thick dark hair and his intense energy, that it was initially unnerving. But working with him felt familiar. After lunch break, Barry led us through a second read-through and discussion before releasing us for the day.

Grocery shopping that night, I passed Michael Learned and F. Murray Abraham in the store. They were both at Williamstown to perform in the other Arthur Miller play on the summer season, THE RIDE DOWN MOUNT MORGAN. They were pushing their grocery carts just like "real people." It felt surreal. I introduced myself to F. Murray, and he said, "I know you," but he couldn't have known me. Still, I was flattered that he saw something in me he thought he knew.

On our second day, rehearsal was moved to a room on the upper level of a school building at Williams College. Picture windows surrounded the space floor to ceiling. It felt like rehearsing in the treetops framed by distant blue mountains.

Company management lost the second housing they'd found for me and my animals, but they had to move us out of the motel. So, at 8:00 p.m. Michael Learned agreed to make space in her rented house for my animals and me, until the theatre found appropriate housing. She and her Boston Bull Terrier named Paloma, Katy and Charlie and I were roomies for a week. We did OK. Charlie had to stay in my bedroom, but Katy and Paloma got along nicely. Michael and I had similar qualities, and she'd played Kate in ALL MY SONS in a PBS production years before. Interestingly, my agent, Jerry Hogan had been her agent once upon a time. Her production of THE RIDE DOWN MOUNT MORGAN was an American premiere and would run simultaneously with our production. One night during the week when I was staying with Michael, she made dinner for me and Patricia Clarkson who was also in THE RIDE DOWN MOUNT MORGAN. I felt so out of place. I felt I wasn't on the same level as these women. And I didn't know how to behave. Same ol' story. Something kept me from being as confident a woman as I was an actress.

At the end of our first week of rehearsals Mr. Miller came to see a run-through of our first act. Near the end of the act, my character has a speech where she describes a dream she had the night before. In the dream, she saw her son who'd been missing in action for years. He was flying his plane high over their house. She'd awakened from her dream to find that the tree they'd planted in his memory, had been struck down by the storm in the night. Her dream, the storm, and the broken tree are a metaphor for the play's story. At the end of the act after I'd delivered the speech, I left the rehearsal stage and walked past Mr. Arthur Miller wearing his University of Michigan ball cap, sitting on the metal folding chair where he'd been watching rehearsal. He grabbed my arm as I passed and smiled at me, "Ya did good, kid." I think I smiled for an hour.

The second Monday in Williamstown after our first week's rehearsal, I was moved to a modern dorm that seemed to have been set down in the middle of a field of tall grass. The apartment in the dorm had windows on all sides, a great kitchen, and a view of those same blue mountains I'd seen from the rehearsal room. I unpacked the car for the first time in a week and a half. Charlie settled into the couch. Katy ran in the field. And I finally relaxed. I realized I was the only person in this long one-level dorm with several empty apartments. It might have been unnerving but for the peacefulness of the place.

The next three nights I sang in the festival's cabaret. The cabaret space had been closed several years for renovation, but this year it was reopening. I realized I was singing in the same cabaret where Kent had sung when he was an intern at Williamstown during his Yale years. He had so loved his summer at Williamstown, and now here I was, not as an intern, but a professional. It is strange how lives intertwine.

Years before, the young Christopher Reeve had also been doing a play at Williamstown when he saw his wife Dana for the first time. She was singing on the cabaret stage. On this night of the cabaret's reopening, Christopher was brought to the newly renovated theatre, and his wheelchair was settled in the back of the house. He hadn't known where he was being taken or what he'd find when he got there. But when the lights went up on the cabaret stage, he must've known he was about to hear his Dana sing the lyric she'd sung the night he first laid eyes on her. "Yours is the only music that makes me dance." It was a touching moment, and truly, there wasn't a dry eye in the house. I sang in a couple of group numbers, and my own solo, Noel Coward's "If Love Were All." It was a deeply affecting evening, and I felt privileged to be part of it. I *was* privileged. The summer of 1996 at Williamstown was a huge gift.

CHAPTER THIRTEEN

williamstown to the roundabout

"Everything that happened seems to be coming back."

Kate Keller, All MY SONS

I carried that gift with me back to the city in the early fall of 1996. Our production of ALL MY SONS at Williamstown had been a great success both with audiences and critics, one of whom called me "a young Katherine Hepburn." The show was so successful that the Roundabout Theatre Company asked to remount the production in New York after the first of the year.

So, Katy and Charlie and I settled back into our routine in Brooklyn Heights. My sweet Westie who was now twelve years old was being treated for a skin condition that had begun in San Diego. The veterinarian we saw there had put her on prednisone, and now she'd been on the drug for three years. I wasn't made aware that extended use of prednisone might be as dangerous to Kathy's health as the skin condition. And back in Brooklyn Heights, Katy began having difficulty walking for more than half a block. I had to carry her the four blocks to and from the vet in our neighborhood. When the elevator in our building went out, which was often, I carried her down and up again the six flights to our apartment. It was no fun for either of us.

But I found an alternative to carrying Katy to the street and back. When the elevator wasn't working, I'd sling her over my shoulder, climb out the fire escape window, and up the half-flight to the roof. It was not very smart, but only slightly dangerous because there was a heavy railing on the fire escape stairs. And when we got to the roof, she could roam free while I watched the sunset. Then I'd clean up after her, and we'd climb down the escape stairs and through the window to the apartment. Only in New York.

I lived my New York actor's life—lunches with friends, auditions, recordings, seeing movies and theatre when anyone could offer a discount. There's a New York truth. Actors unless wealthy, and most of us aren't, can't afford to go to the theatre. Actors can barely afford to live in New York, unless or until they're working. But happily, right now I was.

Sometime after the first of the year, 1997, our production of ALL MY SONS went back into rehearsal. There was a lot of hoopla surrounding the production because it had been so well received in Williamstown, and also because it was the play's fiftieth anniversary. There would be a huge banquet in celebration of the anniversary, and Mr. Miller himself would join the festivities surrounding the opening. The event of this production was so important that the producers felt we needed a star to join the cast. So, our Williamstown Joe Keller, the terrific Joe Costa, was not invited to do the play again. In his place, our new Joe would be John Cullum.

I had fallen in love with John Cullum when I first saw him playing Edward Rutledge in the original Broadway production of 1776 in 1969. And now I'd be playing his wife. Here was another almost unreal situation for me. I had stars in my eyes when I watched John, and yet I could act with him without fear. It's almost as if the inner artist was entirely separate from my outer self. So, I did my work over the next several weeks with two personalities living inside me—the actor and the fan.

The show opened in May of 1997. The Roundabout Theatre Company had not yet moved to its new home—The American Airlines Theatre on Forty-second Street. It was still in the Times Square area but housed in The Criterion Center Stage Right, which had an illustrious history. The theatre building on Forty-fourth and Broadway, originally much larger, began in 1895 as the Oscar Hammerstein Theatre. Then it became The Olympia, then The New York Theatre, then Lowes movie theatre, then another movie theatre called Criterion Theatre which was finally converted again to a live theatre. But critical response to our New York production was not so illustrious as the theatre that housed it. Even with our star, the reception was not what we'd experienced in Williamstown, and not what the producers expected. Here were echoes of my experience with WINGS.

I believe part of the reason was that our production design was almost expressionistic. There were toy planes hanging from the rafters in front of a wide cyclorama, and only an impression of the Keller house. Our costuming was monochromatic. The design made a symbolic statement, not a realistic one. Our Williamstown design had been more realistic, more of the era. So, the audience might have been more easily drawn back into the 1940's. I know the intention of the design was to universalize the story, but taking away the specifics of the era might have done the opposite, might have distanced the audience from the story. And the audience was indeed more distanced from the production. The Criterion was a larger theatre than the intimate space where we'd performed the play in Williamstown.

I was personally criticized for playing Kate in the same way I'd been praised for playing her in Williamstown. For me Kate was the woman behind the man. She was a woman with deep intuition who may have been lying to herself about the reality of her missing son, but she was not deluded and not delicate. She'd often been played as a woman falling apart, but the script supports my interpretation. Arthur Miller's description of her is that she is "... a woman of uncontrolled inspirations, and an overwhelming capacity for love." Her inspirations gave my Kate her strength, and her love kept her focus on others. That's enough defense of my portrayal so far after the fact. But I did have a role model. My parents were businesspeople like the Kellers in the same era, and Mama was most definitely the woman behind the man. I took what I knew of her support of Joe Wilson and plugged it into my Kate's support of Joe Keller.

I can't say I ever truly got to know my New York Joe Keller. John was wonderful to share stage with, but there was no real personal sharing. He'd been a star to me for such a long time, since 1969 watching him sing "Molasses to Rum to Slaves." He blew me away singing that almost-aria. Now he was my acting partner. He certainly didn't play "the star" that he surely was. Oddly, I wish he had. I wish I still held him on a pedestal.

The fall between our Williamstown and New York runs, I'd been summoned to Atlanta by Kenny Leon, now Artistic Director of the Alliance, to play Amanda Wingfield in his production of THE GLASS MENAGERIE. It was my first return to Atlanta since I'd moved to Chicago in the late eighties. Knowing that we'd be remounting ALL MY SONS in New York, I decided it might be a good time to move back to the city I'd never have left if I hadn't felt a responsibility to save my marriage. I felt that now I would have shown the New York casting agents the three areas where they could use me—as a serious singer because of WINGS, as a musical comedy actress because of DAMN YANKEES, and as a dramatic actress because of ALL MY SONS. As much as I loved my Brooklyn Heights apartment, I wanted a bedroom. I wanted to go "home." I felt I could come to New York for auditions and if cast in a show, negotiate housing. It seemed the right and good thing to do.

So, in the early summer of 1997, on a rooftop in downtown Manhattan at our closing party for ALL MY SONS, I shared with the group that I was moving away from the city and back to Atlanta. John said to me, "You don't leave New York when you're at your height in the business!" Then after I explained my reasoning he said, "Well, maybe you're right, but usually you don't leave until your career is on the downswing." Even with John's voice of experience resonating in my ear, when our show closed, I moved to Atlanta. Over the next few years, I would learn the hard way, that John Cullum was right.

CHAPTER FOURTEEN

going home

"Why, we'll do what we will"

Ma Joad, THE GRAPES OF WRATH

After I closed ALL MY SONS, I spent the summer in New York City saying goodbye to friends and theatre people and all the special places I'd loved in the city. When my lease in Brooklyn Heights was up in September, I hired a moving company for the piano and the larger furniture. I packed my Daddy's little Ford Escort hatchback with Katy and Charlie and everything else I owned in the world, then drove to Atlanta—to Sandy Springs to be exact. I'd found a one-bedroom apartment with a balcony online and put down a deposit. The apartment was in a complex just north of the Atlanta city limits off Roswell Road, one of Atlanta's main thoroughfares.

Mama had already checked out the apartment for me. She was so excited I would be living close to her again. After Daddy retired, and my parents had moved to Arkansas and found that they couldn't "go home," they had moved to Atlanta where Kent and I, Lorna and her soon-to-be husband Mark, were all living in the city. So our parents would be among family. But since their move to Atlanta—now years before—Lorna and Mark had moved to Ohio for work, Kent and I had moved to Chicago for work, and Daddy had passed away. So, Mama had been living in the city with no family close by for four years now.

I was glad to be closer to her, but my main pull back to Atlanta was the city itself. It was the only place I'd called home in my adult life. I longed to feel at home again.

My animals and I settled into our new place where Charlie could watch the birds from the balcony and Katy could roam on the long grassy knoll in the center of the apartment complex. After four years of living in virtually one room, this two-bedroom apartment felt palatial. I could sleep in my new bed and exhale more deeply than I had since my Chicago days.

The first month of my move to Atlanta, Kenny Leon, now Artistic Director of the Alliance Theatre, offered me the role of The Nurse in MEDEA for a production to be mounted the following spring. And with his offer of future work, I could relax without worry over when the next paycheck would come. Kenny had given me what felt like an extended vacation. I could see old friends, spend time traveling with Mama to The North Georgia mountains, to Savannah, to the Georgia coastal Islands—Sea and Jekyll and St. Simons. No more waiting for subway trains. No more sculpting my days around train schedules and the time it might take walking city streets to get to this appointment or that. Now I could drive anywhere at any time I wanted. And despite the freeway city that Atlanta had become, constantly clogged with traffic, I was free to sculpt my own time in my own way. The year was capped by a drive to Ohio with Mama in the passenger seat, for a family Christmas at Lorna and Mark's for the first time in years. It was sweet.

Kenny Leon's production of MEDEA in the spring starred the

gracious and beautiful Phylicia Rashad as Medea. I'd asked Kenny if I could switch roles with his wife, Carol Mitchell Leon, who'd been cast as one of the three actresses playing the Greek chorus. The narration of the Greek chorus appealed to the singer in me. And truly, I wasn't ready to play the "old" nurse. I wasn't ready to play an old woman. It was a beautiful production. Phylicia was both sensual and frightening as MEDEA, and Carol brought a depth of wisdom to her Nurse. I was "singing" my role yet again, but I believe for the Greek chorus it was appropriate.

MEDEA was followed by an unexpected offer from Chris Coleman, who'd been my Tom in the production of THE GLASS MENAGERIE that we'd done for Kenny the fall before I'd moved back to Atlanta. Chris was Artistic Director of his Actor's Express, a young progressive theatre company. He asked me if we might apply for a TCG—Theatre Communications Group Artist-in-Residence Grant from Pew Charitable Trust. He was asking me to be in residence at Actor's Express for the 1998-99 season. We applied and were given the grant. We didn't know exactly what I would do with the theatre, but we played our relationship by ear the first months, until eventually I ended up teaching and guiding interns. Also, I was creating a solo theatre piece with Jeff Lunden, based on an Ursula K. Le Guin poem called *Places Names.* Jeff composed a beautiful score for the story with keyboard, winds, percussion and cello. I would narrate the poem. In 2000, a year later, when Chris was made Artistic Director of Portland Center Stage in Oregon, he invited Jeff and me to perform our theatre piece as part of a new play festival called JAW (Just Add Water). Unfortunately, the piece which can't be categorized, never found a home beyond the festival. It was, and remains a big disappointment for me.

In early 1999, during the winter of my residency in Atlanta with Chris, one of my old theatre friends, David Bell, who was now Associate Artistic Director at the Alliance, asked me to play Ma Joad in his production of THE GRAPES OF WRATH. Chris allowed me to split focus during my residency with Actor's Express, so that I could perform in GRAPES. Here I was again, struggling with the idea of playing an old lady. There was no denying that Ma Joad was an old lady. I was in my early fifties now, and I knew that I was truly entering old lady years. So, I began the long process of embracing the passage.

The process has certainly been long. Even now twenty years later, I struggle with being seen as old. At least I'm in good company. I once heard Judi Dench say in an interview "I don't want to play old ladies." But I think she wasn't talking about age in number of years so much as the lack of richness in so many older characters. I suppose that none of us with years of experience wants to play a character that is not as complicated, not as interesting as the women we've become. We all want something to say we can believe in, something to play that feeds us, and that we can feel good about sending out into the universe. But I knew that despite my neurosis over playing old women, Ma Joad is a character to feed the soul. She is a heroine. And it would be a privilege to bring her story to audiences. So, I was happy in rehearsals, till something happened that changed my life.

My sweet Katy had been uncomfortable walking for days. She'd walk a few steps, then fall down. All the years of being treated with prednisone had broken down her little system. But she was still present, and I watched her daily, till one day during tech for GRAPES, she could barely move. This was a ten-out-of-twelve-hour rehearsal day. I'd be gone for twelve hours plus the time it took to drive to and from the theatre. I left that morning knowing I should take her to

The Animal Emergency Center, knowing that she might be close to passing, but I couldn't bring myself to take her to a sterile hospital where she might pass away all alone. So, I sat her down in front of the apartment door, talked to her quietly, told her I'd be back at dinnertime. I told her to wait for me. She sat looking at me as I opened the apartment door and I hoped she understood.

When I got home late that night Katy was waiting for me in the same place where I'd left her, not three feet in front of the door. For the rest of the evening, we communed. She couldn't walk more than a few steps. She didn't want food or water. She only wanted to know I was close. Finally, we spooned on the living room floor and for an hour, maybe longer, I held her while her breathing slowed, then became erratic. At last, her little head raised up, she turned to look me in the eye. I told her it was OK, that she could go. And she did. She left. She was here. Then she was gone. And I wept.

Her passing was a huge loss for me. She'd been with me for fifteen years. She'd seen me through my divorce from Larry, then through his death, then the death of my marriage to Kent, then through our move to Chicago and two apartments there, then our move to New York and two apartments there. Now I'd brought her home to Atlanta where she'd been born. She'd been my companion, my partner. And now she'd let me go. But I wasn't ready to let her go. She understood more about life than I did. She lived until she wasn't living. Even through the pain, she was present. That's what she taught me. Hers was another lesson in presence.

I called my mother after I'd had my first wave of mourning and told her that Katy had passed. I asked if I could bring Katy's body to her house. She said yes. So, I did. Then Mama and I, the farmer's daughter and granddaughter did what we knew to do over the death of a beloved animal. We planted her. Mama and I dug a grave by flashlight in her backyard and placed sweet Katy's body in the earth under Mama's garden. Next day I bought a stone to mark her grave. On the stone is carved "Gentleness."

Done. It was over. What now? Live the next part of life. Play Ma Joad. Finish the residency with Actor's Express. Mourn. With Katy's death I was lost for a while. And though I was grateful for the work, I needed grounding. So, I planted myself more deeply in Atlanta, I bought a condo. And I moved yet again, in the Spring of 1999. I made sure Charlie had a balcony in this lovely old two-bedroom condo in Decatur, Georgia.

We settled in, Charlie and I. He was beginning to fill the space that Katy had left, sitting closer to me on the couch. Sleeping closer on the bed. We'd sit on our new balcony and watch the hummingbirds on the feeder I'd hung from the branch of the Sweet Gum tree overhanging our balcony.

It would be a year before another role would come to me, offered again by the Alliance. But, during that year empty of theatre work, I was back and forth to New York. I had a few auditions for regional theatres in other cities, as well as for a Broadway production of FOLLIES at the Roundabout. This was my first encounter with Stephen Sondheim behind the auditor's table. I was so nervous in front of him, because he's a master, and a hero for me. I knew he'd seen WINGS. He'd actually come to Chicago to see the show, before we moved to New York. But I hadn't met him then. For the FOLLIES audition, I sang "Like it was" from MERRILY WE ROLL ALONG for him, and at the end I did a gesture to "finish" the song. And Mr. Sondheim gave a little laugh and said "Ah, the song with no ending." He smiled at me and gave lovely approval, but I didn't get the job.

None of the jobs I auditioned for during that time did I get, but it was OK, I was keeping my hand in the game. And that was as important as the actual work.

I did have one job though. My recording company, Recorded Books Inc., called me to narrate one of Lee Smith's novels. At that time, they wouldn't allow me to record outside of New York, so I was in touch with actress friend Dana Ivey about staying in her apartment on the upper West side, while she was out of the city working. She said yes and I stayed in her place for the two weeks it took to record the book.

The rest of this year away from theatre was spent adjusting to out-of-work life in Atlanta, which was very different from out-of-work life in New York. Drawing unemployment was trickier. Explaining what it means to be a professional actor to unemployment agencies outside New York, Chicago, and LA is difficult. Actors go in and out of work all the time. We're freelancers. Local agencies don't seem to understand that acting can be an actual profession, unless maybe you're in the movies. I don't know how many times in my life, I've told some official that I'm an actor, and been asked, "Oh, what movies have you been in?" Then they're disappointed when I tell them I'm a stage actor. But I show them my paycheck stubs, and my work history and they begin to believe I'm legitimate, but they never quite understand.

There were fewer professional actors in Atlanta, so opportunities for the spur of the moment coffee get-togethers were fewer. I began to spend more time alone than I had in New York or Chicago. I also began to understand that I'd been changed by my New York/Chicago experiences. I'd been changed by the busyness of the business of working and working to get work. And I didn't seem to know how to live life at a slower pace. I was uncomfortable with so much solitude. Yes, I had good friends and we did get together from time to time. But with the loss of Katy in the city where I'd lost both Larry and Daddy, I was beginning to experience what people mean when they say, "You can't go home again." My own parents hadn't been able to go home to the Arkansas of their youth. Do we ever really learn except through experience?

In the late winter of 2000, I played Hesione Hushabye in George Bernard Shaw's HEARTBREAK HOUSE at The Alliance. It was a truly lovely production. Then after two months of run, it was over. What now? Well now, Tom Key with whom I'd worked in THE GRAPES OF WRATH the year before, asked me to play Emily Dickinson in THE BELLE OF AMHERST at his theatre, The Theatrical Outfit. I of course said yes. THE BELLE OF AMHERST is a one-woman play in which Emily Dickinson tells her life story through her poetry.

On opening night of THE BELLE OF AMHERST, Tom apologized profusely for not having put together an opening night reception. There had been some sort of miscommunication. There were audience members gathered in the lobby to applaud me as I came down the stairs from my dressing room, including my mother, and cousin Phil who'd flown in from Arkansas. But there was no celebration.

Three weeks later, a friend came to see my closing performance. She'd driven me to the theatre that night. And after the performance she came to my dressing room, hugged me, and praised my work. Then she went to get her car while I cleared my dressing room. Tom was there to thank me for my work, but there was no closing night celebration, no champagne, no hoopla. By the time I walked down the stairs to the theatre lobby, it had cleared. I sat down on the wooden file box I'd brought in to use as a prop for the show. I sat in the empty lobby waiting to be picked up by my friend. An incredible wave of sadness enveloped me, and I asked myself, "What am I doing?"

What would I do? I didn't know. And one night sitting alone in my condo, my mother called. She said "Did you call me? I thought I heard you at the front door. Were you here?" Sitting in her condo, she had heard me call her name. But I hadn't been there. I told her, "No. I wasn't there, Mama. But I was thinking about you because I have to tell you something. I can't be here. I don't belong. It was a mistake to come back." And we talked for a long time about what all that meant, how unwise it seemed to move back to New York, but how I felt I had no choice. She listened, asked a few questions, but didn't argue. She didn't tell me not to go.

Not two weeks later, I got a call from Jim Carnahan, now casting director at the Roundabout in New York. He was asking me to audition for the theatre's production of THE MAN WHO CAME TO DINNER which would open their new American Airlines Theatre on Forty-second Street. So, I flew to New York, auditioned for Jerry Zaks, the director. He was unsure about my having moved to Atlanta. I told him if I was cast in the show, I was moving back to New York. I told him I'd moved to Atlanta for some unfinished business, but that was done now so I was coming back.

I suppose there was some truth in that. But the whole truth is that I'd failed to adjust to a different kind of life in Atlanta. I'd failed to accept the changes in myself since I'd lived there seven years before. And to live in Atlanta now, I'd have to accept the changes not only in myself but in the city. I'd failed to even recognize that I was a different woman from the one I'd been those years before. Back in Atlanta, the week after my audition, the Roundabout called to tell me that I was cast in THE MAN WHO CAME TO DINNER which would go into rehearsal that fall.

Looking back on my life, I see now that both moves were foolhardy. A friend of mine recently asked if I had any regrets. I laughed and then said to him, "Haven't you heard that if you have no regrets, you haven't lived?" Well, I surely must have lived, because I have more than a few regrets including both those moves—back to Atlanta, and then back to New York. But when I look more closely, I see that my only real regret is that I had to make both those moves to learn what I needed to know, that you can never go back to any time that's passed. You can't recapture. You might be able to rebuild. But only if you truly want to.

So, now began the business of moving yet again and finding an apartment in New York. Happily, I didn't have to sell my condo right away because a theatre friend needed temporary housing while she sold her own home. She would rent my Atlanta condo, which gave me the freedom to concentrate on finding an apartment in the city. I flew back to New York and gave myself a weekend to find a one-bedroom apartment for under $1000 which at that time was unheard of. But I found it in Kensington Brooklyn, south of Park Slope on the F train. The F line had no express, so the trip from Times Square would take an hour, no matter the time of day. Still, I'd found my apartment in a weekend which was also unheard of. I flew back to Atlanta, hired another moving company, said goodbye to my Mama which was not easy for either of us because I was leaving her in Atlanta alone again. I was hoping that when I became more successful, when I started making more money, I'd bring Mama to live closer to me. Those were my wishes. I would learn the hard way, that my wishes were nothing but pipe dreams.

backtracking

"Sometimes a small role is just a small role."

Anne Bancroft

Things moved very quickly now. I packed my apartment for the moving truck, packed the car with my personals including my Charlie, and got on the road. I drove into Kensington, Brooklyn on April Fool's Day of 2000, which in hindsight seems appropriate. The moving truck would arrive the next day. I found a place to park on Caton Avenue, the street where I'd be living, and unpacked my Daddy's little hatchback. I set up Charlie's litter box, food and water, then I crossed the street to buy a few staples at a convenience market, the only store in sight. I bought coffee and breakfast makings and a frozen food dinner. Back in the apartment I unpacked the bathroom, put a few things I'd brought for the kitchen into the cupboards, ate dinner, then fell asleep on a palate on the living room floor of my new apartment. I discovered pretty quickly that Caton Avenue was a truck route. Truckers would double-park in front of my building, motor still idling, while they ran into the store across the street to pick up something for the road. But my apartment was on the third floor, and the bedroom was in the back of the railroad track-style apartment away from the street, where much of the noise would be muffled. I would be fine.

Again, I'd found a nice space to live. Large rooms, wood floors, big kitchen with room for table and chairs, and a long hallway from the front door that opened into a kind of central foyer off which all the other rooms fanned. This central space that wasn't a hall and wasn't a room was the heart of the apartment and was big enough to hold my Yamaha Clavinova and the hutch that Kent and I had bought together years before. It had been with me since our Atlanta days. The apartment was nice enough, but the neighborhood, not so much.

This was a very old building in a very old section of Brooklyn, in a neighborhood with virtually no conveniences except for the small store across Caton Ave. and the laundromat next to it. I would use that laundromat more often than the laundry room in the basement of my building. It spooked me. It reminded me a little of the basement laundry room in *Rosemary's Baby*. The neighborhood where I'd chosen to live was residential and had once been a grand area of Brooklyn. The residents now were primarily Russian and Eastern European, with a smattering of us Manhattan transplants who couldn't afford to live in the city because by this time the dot-commers had invaded Manhattan and upped the price of renting throughout the city. It felt safe and comfortable once I was in the apartment, but getting to and from shopping would be a chore. To get to better grocery stores, I'd have to walk four city blocks and take the subway to Park Slope, one stop closer to Manhattan. I bought my first rolling cart for carrying groceries and sundries, so I could more easily schlep it all back to Kensington on the train. Getting to and from the city would also be a chore. My solace was work, and I did have work almost immediately, thanks to Recorded Books, Inc.

This was the time period when I narrated *Gone with the Wind*. The company's studios were in Midtown Manhattan, and so from mid-April through June, three days a week I'd take the train to record a three-hour session. My train ride and the walk to and from the studio was nearly as long as the session itself. But I was grateful for the work and for the time to acclimate to this new paradigm of living in the city I'd given myself.

My next work started in June, overlapping the final sessions for *Gone with the Wind*. It was the job that had brought me back to the city — The Roundabout Theatre's production of the 1940's play, THE MAN WHO CAME TO DINNER by Moss Hart and George S. Kaufman. The theatre's offices and rehearsal rooms were also in Midtown where I would share work for a time with a very gifted cast of New York actors. Harriet Harris, Byron Jennings, Lewis Stadlen, wonderful Bill Duell and beautiful Ruby Holbrook both of whom have left us, fourteen more cast members, and our stars—Nathan Lane and Jean Smart. One of the other cast members was my good friend Terry Beaver with whom I'd be sharing stage for the first time since we'd worked together in 1981 on a production of WHOSE LIFE IS IT ANYWAY? at The Alliance in Atlanta. Now we were cast as Mr. and Mrs. Stanley, the owners of the house where the man comes to dinner.

Three years earlier, in the late Spring of 1997, Terry and I had both been performing in The Theatre District. I at The Criterion in ALL MY SONS, and Terry at The Helen Hayes in THE LAST NIGHT OF BALLYHOO. This was Terry's first play in New York. The play had premiered in Atlanta the fall before, and at first Terry was reluctant to transfer with the production to New York. But he finally said "yes" and it was good, because he'd made such a splash on Broadway that he was nominated for a Tony as best featured actor in a play, for his performance in BALLYHOO. I was able to see his show before mine went into performance, and he was so very fine in his production. I felt proud for him. The Tony Award Ceremonies were held on Sunday evening, June 1. Terry asked me to accompany him to the ceremony, and I was honored to be asked. After our matinees that Sunday, Terry and I were picked up at our respective theatres and driven to the celebration in a limo ordered for him by the BALLYHOO producers. We walked the red carpet while fans behind the velvet ropes called and applauded the actors as we passed into Radio City Music Hall. I felt privileged to be asked to share Terry's special honor on that night of the fifty-first Tony Awards. I *was* privileged.

Now in 2000, working with Terry for the first time since 1981 was again special for me. Our large cast of actors was a terrific group of pros. Jean Smart is the classiest of women. Nathan Lane was nothing but kind to me. Being costumed by designer William Ivey Long was itself an adventure. My character, Daisy Stanley is the first character the audience sees. She begins the play alone onstage. William Ivey told me that first costumes, especially women's, are the most important. He said if you get them right, audiences will forgive less-impressive costumes as the show moves along. But my costume wasn't quite right. After only a couple of previews William Ivey said the color was wrong. The dress was a gorgeous rusty brown, but against the browns of the set, the dress disappeared. His intention was to show Daisy as an extension of her home, but she was such an extension that she blended in. So, he built another dress, this one made of a rich dark blue fabric. Same design, but now the color popped in front of the browns of the set. I have to say that though my character was a little slow on the uptake, she certainly knew how to dress. I felt beautiful in the costume.

My character was a sort of discombobulated type, and when I'd auditioned for Jerry Zaks, Jim Carnahan had said to me, "Do that thing you do." I remember him saying, "Not that other thing you do, but you know the one I mean." Well, I'm not sure I did know what thing I did that he was referring to. But I reached into my bag of past characters and pulled out one that might have been an older version of my Philia from A FUNNY THING HAPPENED ON THE WAY TO THE FORUM. She was lovely but not quite present in the real world. My Daisy was a kind of caricature, which is not what I do best, but I thought it was what was being asked, because my audition got me the job.

But now, well after the fact, I think I may have been cast, at least in part, out of respect for the long-departed Larry Shue. Jerry Zaks had directed Larry's THE FOREIGNER when it premiered off-Broadway. He knew I'd been Larry's wife. I'm sure Jim Carnahan was promoting me, but I believe that being Larry's ex-wife might have influenced Jerry Zak's thinking. I also believe he thought I was a little crazy because of my move away from New York and then back again. He wasn't entirely wrong. After my audition, he'd questioned me seriously about how I was doing. Was I sure I was going to be able to see the show through? No one had ever questioned my professionalism, but I could see that he was unsure about me. So, when I was offered the role days later, I was surprised. But I was also grateful because it was a sign that moving back to New York was the right thing to do.

What I did not understand was that in accepting the role of Daisy Stanley, I might be knocking myself down a rung or two on the "show-biz ladder." I'm not sure I even knew there was a show-biz ladder. But there is a hierarchy in theatre, and I'd always landed on a higher rung of the ladder. I was about to experience what it meant to perch at a lower level. The perfect metaphor for the invisible ladder is the assignment of dressing rooms.

The old Selwyn Theatre on Forty-second Street had opened in 1918. Years later it had been converted to a movie house, then stood dark for many years until now it had been refurbished and reopened as The Roundabout's new home. It's dressing rooms flanked the landings of a zig-zag staircase off stage right. My room was off the very top landing of the staircase. I shared the room with two other actresses, Kit Flanagan and Julie Halston, who has since climbed the showbiz ladder more than a few rungs. Nathan's and Jean's dressing rooms were of course on stage-level. The other actors were assigned rooms up the staircase according to role size, how much stage time the character had. It makes sense that the smaller the role, the less time onstage, the farther away the dressing room. Daisy Stanley was not nearly so large or demanding a role as any of the other three I'd played in New York. The role was not insignificant, but by accepting the offer to play Daisy, I was in effect announcing to New York casting agents that I'd accept smaller roles than those I'd played up until then. I don't agree with the adage, "There are no small roles, only small actors." There are certainly small actors. But there are indeed small roles.

You just have to remember when you accept any role, why you're accepting. And I'd accepted Daisy Stanley not because I wanted to play the role, and not because I wanted to be in this important production that would re-open the old Selwyn Theatre, and not even because it would bring me again to New York where I could go back to living the life I thought I was supposed to be living. I took the role because I didn't know what else to do. There it is. I hadn't known why I was taking the role, but I didn't know what else to do. That's a precarious reason for doing anything. I learn my life lessons slowly.

In rehearsal, working on Daisy Stanley I was following to the letter what I believed Jerry Zaks wanted of me. At the end of the second week of rehearsal, we'd been doing run-throughs for several days. The final run-through of this second week was performed for Moss Hart's wife, Kitty Carlisle Hart, and Anne Kaufmann Schneider, George S. Kaufman's daughter. At the end of the run-through that day, Mrs. Hart and Mrs. Schneider had a long conference behind closed doors with Jerry Zaks. The rest of us waited and wondered what was being said. And when the two women left, the 90-year-old Mrs. Hart tripped on the transom of the rehearsal room door and fell. She wasn't badly hurt, but it seemed like some kind of omen.

Once they'd left, Jerry pulled the cast together and told us basically we had to go back to square one and rework the entire show, especially the top of the show. He said, "Because you're not talking and listening to one another." And the top of the show was my only real scene. Then as the cast was leaving for the day, he asked both me and Jean Smart to wait, and when everyone else had gone, he spoke to me first. He pulled me behind a rehearsal set piece. We were squeezed between the wall and the flat. It was very uncomfortable and odd. Then he said to me, "You seem so sad, and I'd like to know why?" It was not an empathetic question. He was irritated with me. That let me know that Mrs. Hart and Mrs. Schneider had pointed to my performance as part of the problem. I was embarrassed that those two important women of the theatre saw me doing work that wasn't up to their standards, much less my own.

I told Jerry Zaks that I was doing what I thought he wanted, that it was embarrassing to be told I needed to be honest onstage because normally, that's what I did best. But I knew I wasn't doing what I did best, I was dancing on the surface of the role. I was following his orders, at least I thought I was, and I told him that normally I played more complex roles, and I couldn't seem to find my way into this one, that I felt shackled. "Shackled?!" he said to me. The word had unsettled him. He didn't realize how controlled I'd felt. And I know I wasn't alone in that feeling, but I didn't dare share that. He was quiet for a few moments, then finally said, "Take some advice from Anne Bancroft. Sometimes a small role is just a small role."

Jerry Zaks told me to not worry, he'd fix it, and to trust him. But I didn't know how to trust him. I didn't understand his direction and I never broke out of the shackles. I realize now they were partly of my own making. I should never have accepted the role as my re-introduction to New York theatre. I was operating yet again in survival mode. My mother would come to New York and see the show the night it was filmed for PBS on Saturday, October seventh. I'm disappointed that of all the roles I played in New York, the one that was filmed is the one I can't be proud of.

So, from rehearsals in June till the closing of THE MAN WHO CAME TO DINNER on October twenty-sixth, 2000, I'd ride the F train to Times Square, do my play, then ride the train back to Kensington. When it arrived at my stop, I would get off the back of the train because after midnight the gates at the front were locked. My four-block walk became an eight-block walk to my building at night, through empty, unlit streets. I was always apprehensive on the walk home from the train at night, so I'd walk quickly. And one night trying to cut my walk short, I climbed a hillock, slid on wet grass and fell. I wasn't hurt so much as stunned, but I couldn't move. I didn't get up. I just sat there. I sat on the hillock for a long time, and let myself cry. I looked at the darkened buildings surrounding me, and asked myself, "What have I done?"

I was beginning to realize what I'd done by moving back to New York. I'd not only knocked myself down the showbiz ladder, I'd raised my cost of living while lowering my standard of living. Every home I'd had before then was beautiful—in Atlanta, Chicago, Brooklyn Heights, and Atlanta again. But there was nothing beautiful about this place where I lived now. It was serviceable, safe, yes, once I was inside. But everything was colored a dark gray/brown from the exhaust of the trucks driving by on Caton Avenue. The buildings, the streets, the apartment itself was gray.

One afternoon, I was riding in the dirty, always smelly elevator in my apartment building with an older Russian lady who'd lived there for years. She was talking about the mice in her apartment that management couldn't seem to get rid of, when suddenly she turned to me and said, "Don't be like me. I hope you get out of this place before you die." My God. She was reading my mind.

At least I still had wheels. I had the freedom to leave the city whenever I wanted in my Daddy's little Ford Escort. Then one night walking home late after the show, just beyond my building's entrance I saw the back end of a car sitting in the middle of the street. As I walked closer, I thought "No, it can't be." But it was. It was my car. Somebody had sideswiped my father's little car, dragged it halfway into the street, and run. No note. It was totaled. I could see that. I called the police. I waited for the city to come tow the car. I asked what could be done to find whoever did it. And the policeman said to me, "Sorry. Nothing." There went my wheels. There went my freedom. There was nothing I could do but stand next to my little broken hatchback in the middle of Caton Avenue and wait for the city truck to come tow it away. What else could I do? What had I done?

despair

What I had done was put myself in the position of having to take every job that might come along. There would be no leeway for me to pick and choose work. I'd have to take every possible job that was presented. Up until now nearly every show I'd done was not a job done simply for money. I had managed to attract the work that I was proud and happy to do no matter the money. Money always came, often just in time, often no more than needed, but money had always come. Now, I had sacrificed my possibility of home and extended theatre family in Atlanta on the altar of possible success once again in "the big time." I didn't believe my choice to come back to New York had been that shallow, but I now believe that partly, it had been. I felt I'd betrayed myself. And I was deeply unhappy.

But the heart of my move back to New York was more complicated than reestablishing myself in "the big time." I'd felt that the Atlanta theatre community didn't recognize my accomplishments in New York and Chicago, and how huge those experiences had been for me. I knew in my heart though, that the person I was asking recognition from most of all, was and always had been my mother.

The mistake I made moving back to Atlanta was in not realizing how deeply my need for my mother's understanding of my work, was coiled around my sense of responsibility for her. Yes, I wanted to go back to the city where I'd lived and worked in my heyday, but I now understood that I also went back out of a sense of duty to Mama. It would've been much smarter for me and ultimately for her, to go back to Chicago, the city that had launched me to New York, where I might eventually bring her to live near me. I came to understand that neither the move back to Atlanta, nor the move back to New York had brought the personal recognition I was so in search of. And now that I was in foreign territory in both the business and in my home life, I fell into a depression as dark gray as the neighborhood where I was living. I did the worst possible thing I could've done for myself, I started drinking daily. Again. I knew I needed help. So, I looked for another therapist, and found a man named Ira. His name means "he who watches," and for the next several years, he would keep watch over me. And I was helped. Yet again.

The winter of 2000 was barren. There was no work to audition for. Nothing was coming along, until finally, one show presented itself. It was a musical version of WHATEVER HAPPENED TO BABY JANE? Oh no! I prayed I wouldn't have to take this job. I hated the movie. I hated what those two celebrated, gifted actresses had to put themselves through. And now they'd made a musical version of the film, and because there was no other job on the horizon, I told my agents to give me a few days to think about the audition. They wanted me to audition for Blanche, the Joan Crawford role. Not only did I not want to put that story out into the universe, I couldn't imagine stuffing my psyche into the role. But I needed a job. So, I thought about it. I felt had no choice but to think about it. I put my agents off for a week. Then just when I was about to tell them to set up the audition, an angel in the form of Philip Himberg descended.

Philip was the Artistic Director of the outdoor summer theatre at Sundance Institute in Utah, home of the Sundance Film Festival. This was a summer theatre program that no longer exists, but then was still producing one musical every summer in their outdoor theatre. Philip had asked my agents if I might consider playing Rosie, Fanny's mother in FUNNY GIRL with wonderful Judy Blazer as Fanny Brice.

He didn't need me to audition, just to take a meeting. So, when I walked into the audition room and Philip told me how much he liked my work and asked would I like to come to Utah for the summer, I told him I'd like nothing better. And there it was. I was given work that rescued me at the eleventh hour. Yet again.

CHAPTER SIXTEEN

sundance

"Who taught her everything she knows?"

Rosie Brice, FUNNY GIRL

WHen Rosie Brice in the musical of FUNNY GIRL asks that question, she is talking about her talented daughter, Fanny. And who taught me everything I know? My Rosie Brice, Bess Wilson. I never thought of my Mama as being a stage mother, but she was there all along the way watching virtually every performance I gave, in church basements, behind pulpits, on stages small and large, in regional theatres all over the country and on Broadway. She was there for over forty of my fifty years of performing.

Before my career ever began, Mama was taking thanks for my solos in church. I remember standing behind her at the end of a service while she received compliments from people lined up to congratulate her on her talented daughter. Truth is, I hated it. I didn't want congratulations for my performance, I wanted the audience to feel what I felt in the moment I was singing. I wanted them to be moved. And then I wanted to disappear. I once read that Madeline Kahn had said, as a child she wanted to "be the music." So did I. When I sang, I was the music. Mama never understood that. She only knew my performing was important to people, that I looked pretty, and sang like an angel. At least, that's how my eight-year-old self saw it. I knew she was proud of me. But she didn't understand that singing was my work. She couldn't understand that I was singing not so much for approval or attention, but for connection—the connection I felt to something larger than myself when I sang, and the responsibility I felt to the people I was singing for. She may have been right when she'd once said to me "You oughtta be a preacher." So, maybe she did understand. It's just that what was important to her was different from what was important to me.

Mama was not a cookie-baking type. She was driven by a need to get ahead. She was a motivator. She was a performer in "the real world." She liked to dress. She liked to decorate her home. She knew how to present herself to people. She was a born hostess. She liked to take care of household business and was a partner to Daddy in his business. And in those ways, she protected her home and family. She did like to pretend she knew more than she actually did. Reader's Digest was Mama's magazine. She knew just enough about what was going on in the world to carry on conversations. But not too deeply.

When I played ingenues in musicals in my twenties, it was easy for Mama to share her feelings with me, to understand what she saw me do. But when more complicated roles began to come along, Mama wasn't quite sure how to respond. When I played my final Gertrude and was nearly raped by my Hamlet in the closet scene, Mama was disturbed, and she struggled with what to say. I don't remember what she told me, but I do remember the discomfort of it. And like in other situations, she backed away from her real feelings to come up with something she thought was acceptable like "That was very complicated." But more often than not, she'd simply say, "It was a good show."

When years later I realized that my Mama had been living through me without fully understanding my work, it made me sad, or mad, or it made me try too hard to make her understand. I'd much rather she'd have told me she didn't understand, or that she didn't like what she saw or asked why I took the role. No, her response remained focused on how she was perceived. She'd be too embarrassed to admit that she didn't understand or didn't like something she thought was important, because other people praised my work. What made my work important was other people's opinions. Maybe not entirely, but praise from others legitimized me, and so I believe legitimized her. At least it felt that way.

I wish I'd known my mother's deeper heart, but I could never get fully inside her. She seemed to hold a secret in some private place that I never furrowed out. But whatever her secret, she has surely informed all the mothers I've played. Truth is, she's informed every role I've played because she gave me her performer spirit. Hard as it sometimes is for me to admit, Bess Wilson absolutely taught me everything I know.

* * *

The summer of 2001 was nothing but a joy. Those of us cast in the production of FUNNY GIRL were flown from New York City to Salt Lake City. Each of us was given a new rental car, directions to Orem, Utah, and to the apartment complex where we were each given two-bedroom apartments for the summer. The little town of Orem sits at the base of the mountain that is home to the Sundance Institute, and to the outdoor theatre where we'd perform our play.

The summer was a working vacation for all of us. And I made a lifelong friend in Judy Blazer who was a brilliant Fanny Brice. She's an extraordinary singer and a beautiful woman inside and out. Our lives have gone in different directions but when we're in touch, it's as if no time has passed. We have the kind of bond that so many actors develop while running a show. We might never work together again but we've become family, and that deep attachment never goes away.

A "real world" friend of mine believes that actors are selfish. I think it's true that we're self-involved. But selfish? No more than most human beings. As a matter of fact, actors are some of the most generous people I know. As a tribe we are self-aware, because we are our own raw material. We might be neurotic, if neurotic means worrying over things that are not real. But then, things that are not real are at the center of our creativity. And that center is imagination. I do love actors. I love being one of them. But selfish? I don't think so.

Of all the mothers I've played, I believe that Rosie Brice may have been the mother most closely related to my own mother. Rosie was the solo mother of a performing daughter after she separated from her husband. And my mother was solo for twenty-seven years after my father died. Mama was a girlfriend. She had a group of women she enjoyed hanging out with, much like Rosie Brice's card-playing neighbors. My mother was a businesswoman like the real Rosie Brice—Rose Borach was her actual name. She bought and sold real estate. She managed the saloons that she and her husband owned. My mother worked together with my father helping him manage the wholesale leather business he'd bought in his sixties. And it happened that Rosie Brice was the last mother my mother saw me play.

Mama had waited to come to see our show at Sundance till the final week of our three-month contract because I needed help flying with my two cats. I'd acquired another kitty before I left New York, from the local vet in Brooklyn, a little Mama cat. The Vet had found homes for all her kittens but no one wanted the Mama. So, she ended up living with Charlie and me. We named her Daisy. The airline would allow a person to fly with only one animal. Another actress in our show had taken responsibility for Daisy on the flight from New York to Utah, while I'd handled Charlie. And since I still had a sublettor in my New York apartment, at the end of our run at Sundance, I decided to fly back to Atlanta with Mama and the cats, for a brief rest before my next job was to begin at The Milwaukee Rep.

A month before I'd left New York for Utah, Joe Hanreddy, then artistic director of The Rep had flown me to Milwaukee to audition for Lillian Garrett Groag and her play called, THE MAGIC FIRE. The play was to be part of the Rep's 2001/02 season. Joe thought I'd be good for the grandmother in the piece, because he'd seen me play in DRIVING MISS DAISY a few years before. Lillian didn't see me in that role, but she gave me another role in the play. So, thanks to Joe's bringing me to Milwaukee for the audition, I'd have a long block of work from Summer at Sundance through Fall at The Rep.

I'd come to think of The Milwaukee Rep as one of my theatre homes. I loved the city of Milwaukee. I'd gathered a few friends over the twenty years I'd worked at The Rep as an out-of-towner, and I'd been given some wonderful roles on Rep stages through the years. Besides Daisy in DRIVING MISS DAISY, I'd played nine other roles for The Rep.

And of course, I'd been taken with the production of OUR TOWN, to The Omsk State Drama Theatre in Omsk, Siberia to perform our play on a Russian Stage for Russian audiences. And that may have been the most extraordinary experience of my life. Yes, The

Milwaukee Rep had been a true theatre home for me.

At the end of the Sundance summer, Mama and I flew with the cats to Atlanta. Then I took a quick trip to New York and back, to check in on my subletter and my apartment. It was an absolute mess. I'd been wary of this young Australian hairdresser before I left for Utah, and I should've followed my intuition and not let him take the apartment. He'd brought in a roommate which wasn't part of our deal. He'd broken some of my things. He'd broken into my desktop computer and communicated as me on some gay porn sites. My plants were virtually dead, and the apartment was filthy. He'd paid rent while I was gone, but my apartment was trashed. And I felt violated. I *was* violated. I ousted him and went to work cleaning and putting my space back in order. I decided not to find another subletter for my time working at The Rep. I flew back to Atlanta for a couple of weeks rest. Then Tuesday of my second week back, the world changed. It was Tuesday, September eleventh, 2001.

On the morning of 9/11, I was getting ready for my day. I was putting on makeup at the little vanity off the bedroom that had been my father's. I was listening to NPR on the little boom box I'd brought from New York for my out-of-town gigs. And just after 8:45 a.m. regular programming was interrupted with the special report that an airplane had just crashed into the North Tower of the World Trade Center. I couldn't believe what I'd heard and called out for my mother who'd been downstairs watching TV. She'd seen the report at the same time I'd heard it. She was already on her way upstairs. We turned on the little TV in my father's bedroom. We sat on Daddy's bed and watched the news as it was happening. We thought this must've been a plane that lost power, or lost communication with the flight tower. But when less than twenty minutes later we watched as the second plane flew into the South tower, we knew. The whole world knew that this was an attack.

My mother said, "I felt that!" She sounded like a little girl. She was surprised that she'd viscerally felt the plane crash into the tower. I remember being irritated with her, because I thought, "Of course you did. Everybody did. This is not about you!" She was afraid. Of course, she was. I remember that what I felt initially was "How dare they!" My fear showed up as anger. Mama's fear was that of a child's.

We stayed in my father's bedroom for the entire day, watching as the ABC news anchor, Peter Jennings, delivered the frightening events as they unfolded, with grace and courage and remarkable skill. I was grateful for all the newscasters that day, and how they handled with such calm each unbelievable new bit of information. That day, they served as anchors not only for the news, but for our spirits.

CHAPTER SEVENTEEN

the next work 2001

"Nobody knows nothin'. Ever."

Maddelena, THE MAGIC FIRE

Rehearsals at The Milwaukee Rep were to begin only a week after 9/11. Because I couldn't fly by myself with two cats, I'd decided to rent a car and drive from Atlanta to Milwaukee. But my mother insisted that I take her Oldsmobile Cutlass Sierra. It was the first car she'd bought on her own after my father died. She'd recently bought another car and wanted to give me the '96 Olds, so I took it with thanks. Another family car. It gave me a sense of protection since my father's car had been totaled. Cars and leather shoes had always been important in our family. My father had given me my first car when I was in college, a light blue Dodge Dart, and he'd always made sure we had good shoes. Good leather shoes. These were the gifts of the shoe repairman, the traveling salesman, the owner of a wholesale leather company that my father had been. And now my mother was continuing that tradition by offering me the car she'd bought on her own as an independent woman. The car was important to me. It represented my mother, my father, and the traveling work life. It seemed right that I'd be driving a family car on the way to my next work.

On the first day of rehearsal at The Rep we were all grateful to have the work, now that we were living in a very different, precarious world. The title of our play, THE MAGIC FIRE seemed to counterbalance the dark fire that had taken down the towers. This production would be one of the most beautiful I'd ever walk inside. The lights enfolding this memory piece of an Argentinian family were golden. They glowed. They transformed the set and the actors into a sepia moving picture. Everything about the production seemed to shine from within. It was a physically beautiful production of the beautiful true story of our director/playwright, Lillian Garrett-Groag's childhood in Argentina. I am grateful to have been a part of it.

When the show closed it was early November, and I'd been out of town for five months, I was ready to sleep in my own bed. So, Daisy and Charlie and I drove out of Milwaukee in Mom's Oldsmobile Cutlass Sierra on our way to Kensington, Brooklyn for the first time since 9/11 changed our world.

I took the Southern route through Pennsylvania and New Jersey across Staten Island to the Verrazano Narrows Bridge. And as I drove over the narrows, I could see to the North, lower Manhattan. And it was burning. Now two months after the tragedy, smoke was still rising from ground zero. And I felt afraid.

I continued driving East into Brooklyn, carrying with me this eerie feeling. I drove north to Kensington and the apartment I called home. I found a parking space near the entrance of my building on Caton Avenue. I carted the two cats and their paraphernalia up the elevator to the apartment. I set up their food and water on the kitchen floor. In late August when I'd come back to oust the irresponsible subletter, I'd left the windows cracked open to air the place out. And now I saw on the kitchen counters what looked like a slight coat of dust. I dragged my finger across the countertop and realized that it wasn't dust from the exhaust of trucks passing on Caton Avenue. It was ash that had been blown on the wind from West to East, from Manhattan to Brooklyn. My apartment was covered in a fine layer of ash from the fires that had burned the towers and the people in them. My apartment had been anointed with the ash from the tragedy. I sank to the kitchen floor and began to sob. I wept hard. I don't know for how long.

My god. I'd experienced 9/11 from a distance along with the rest of the country. But not until I was near it, did I fully feel it. And now, the tragedy was present in my home. My home. Home. Was this home? Had it ever been? It didn't feel like home. It felt like yet another out-of- town apartment where I'd created a comfortable space for the time it took to do the work and then move on.

What now? Do the work in front of me. Unpack the car. Clean the apartment. Clean the apartment again. Call my friends, my agents, the casting people. Begin again the life of the out-of-work New York actor. Set up coffees and lunches. Go on auditions. See theatre when I could afford it. Wait for the next work. What else was there to do?

the next work 2002

"Sundays...when things were beautiful."

The Old Lady, SUNDAY IN THE PARK WITH GEORGE

And the work in 2002 was unexpectedly beautiful. First, I was called back to Atlanta in the late winter and was given yet again, without audition, another role. This time Mrs. Higgins in MY FAIR LADY, at Atlanta's Theatre of the Stars. It was a shared production with Dallas Summer Musicals in Texas. From Eliza to Mrs. Higgins. I'd come full circle. From ingenue to old lady.

And the next old lady would be one I would never forget, in one of the most wonderful theatrical experiences of my life. I was cast as The Old Lady, George's mother, in SUNDAY IN THE PARK WITH GEORGE. The production would be part of the Sondheim Celebration at the Kennedy Center which would include the remounting of six Stephen Sondheim musicals. The first half of the summer, SUNDAY IN THE PARK WITH GEORGE would run in rep with COMPANY and SWEENEY TODD. During the second half of the summer, PASSION, A LITTLE NIGHT MUSIC, and MERRILY WE ROLL ALONG would run in rep. There was also a local high school production of INTO THE WOODS, and a Japanese production of PACIFIC OVERTURES.

Mandy Patinkin would do his solo Sondheim show. And the great Barbara Cook would sing her Mostly Sondheim Concert. It was a fifteen-week repertory festival in honor of Sondheim's musicals. The summer was affectionately referred to as Camp Sondheim.

During this summer celebration of his work, then seventy-one-year-old Stephen Sondheim seemed perpetually happy. These were re-mountings of his musicals that had long since been proven, so he was free to enjoy the process and everyone involved. He was free to move from rehearsal to rehearsal, participate when he wanted and observe when he didn't. He was free to go out with us after rehearsals. He was free to have fun. He was free to bask in the adoration. And he *was* adored. He worked individually with the leads in each of the shows. I was jealous of our leads, Raul Esparza as George and Melissa Erico as Dot, who got to work one on one with "the master."

Chris Groenendaal who had played Anthony in the original SWEENEY TODD and had also been in the original Broadway production of SUNDAY IN THE PARK WITH GEORGE was playing Jules in our production. Flo Lacey who'd played the title role in EVITA for many years touring the world, was playing Yvonne in our production. Neither Chris nor Flo nor I had been called to work with Steve, as we called Mr. Sondheim. But on the day of our opening, we all three were summoned to meet with him. No one had said why we were summoned, only that Mr. Sondheim wanted to meet with us in the rehearsal room at the Kennedy Center at 1:00. Oh my god, we thought we might be fired. That was a kneejerk reaction. It was highly unlikely. But to be called on opening day for a rehearsal with the composer with whom we hadn't worked during the entire rehearsal process, was highly unusual and very scary. Would he cut our songs, or parts of them? What was this about?

He called Chris and Flo into the room first, and I waited the interminable half hour till they came out of the room. I didn't have time to ask what had gone on because I was immediately ushered into the room where Steve greeted me warmly. He asked me to sing for him from Raul's and my duet, BEAUTIFUL, so I began singing. When I got to the lyric, "Going all the stillness, the solitude…" he stopped me. He asked me to sing that phrase again. So, I did.

And he said "Stop. There it is. 'Solitude,' That's a triplet, yes?"

"Yes."

"It's an eighth note triplet not a quarter note triplet. One more time."

I sang it again this time with an eighth note triplet.

And he said, "That's it."

And I said, "That's it?"

"Yes, that's all. That's it."

Then he thanked me, told me how much he was enjoying my performance and our production. And I told him how much I loved being part of the celebration, how much I loved his music.

And that *was* it. He'd only wanted the rhythm he had written to match the word he had chosen to be sung as he had written it. That was what he wanted. Clarity. Stephen Sondheim has written that the principles that guide his work are all in service of clarity, without which nothing else matters. His clarity mattered so much to me. That was my lesson from "the master."

* * *

In the Fall of 2002, I was back again in Atlanta for a play at The Alliance called FRAME 312. It was a play by Keith Reddin based on the true events surrounding the Kennedy assassination, and the controversial frame in the famous Zapruder film just before the first shot was fired. When I was in Atlanta doing Mrs. Higgins earlier in the year, Susan Booth the new artistic director at The Alliance had asked me to audition for the central role in FRAME 312, and she gave me the role. So, I knew in the winter I'd be working in the fall as well. What I hadn't known yet was that I'd also be singing Sondheim in the summer at the Kennedy Center. The year 2002 gave me six months of back-to-back work. A blessing.

During rehearsals for FRAME 312, I was called back to New York for a one-day marathon rehearsal and performance at Avery Fisher Hall in Lincoln Center. I'd been asked to sing in The Sondheim Celebration Concert, a benefit for The Kennedy Center. Steve had asked several of us to come sing our songs from the summer's productions. I was honored to be asked to sing the duet BEAUTIFUL with Raul Esparza.

On a Sunday night after rehearsal for FRAME 312 in Atlanta, I was flown to New York. My good friend Rosemary Prinz had offered me her apartment on West End Avenue while she was out of town working. On Monday morning, thirty-two of us—twenty-six actor/singers, and six conductors gathered in a rehearsal room at Lincoln Center. We were quickly divided into soprano, alto, tenor and bass, told where to sit, and were handed the music for two group numbers, "A Weekend in the Country" from A LITTLE NIGHT MUSIC which would open the second act of the concert, and "Sunday" from SUNDAY IN THE PARK WITH GEORGE, which would close the evening's concert. Being in the room with all those musical theatre pros, working together quickly to learn this music that we'd perform only once that evening, was thrilling!

After we'd learned the numbers, we were taken to the concert hall, given our show order, our entrances and exits, and told which mikes to use. Then one by one we went through the show, top to bottom. We sang our pieces only once in front of this phenomenal full orchestra of musicians also rehearsing together for the first time.

Then around 6:00 we went our separate ways to get ready for the evening. I went back to Rosemary's which luckily was only blocks away. I had a little something to eat, put on my makeup and my show clothes, walked back to Lincoln Center, and found my assigned dressing room by 7:30 half hour.

Then at 8:00 the overture to MERRILY WE ROLL ALONG began, conducted by celebrated arranger Jonathan Tunick. And we were off. I was standing backstage left, early, waiting in the wings and watching Christine Baranski quietly go through her number, "The Worst Pies in London." She'd played Mrs. Lovett in SWEENEY TODD the summer before. She was in the scary position of performing first in the evening. But when she hit stage and the audience roared for her beloved self, she dazzled, and got the show off to a running start. Raul and I were seventh on the program of thirty numbers, very early in the evening. And when it was our turn, we did well. The response to our duet was lovely. So, now I could relax and watch everyone else. An article about the concert by Stephen Holden in the New York Times two weeks later said that "Beautiful, an exquisite ballad was wonderfully performed by Linda Stephens and Raul Esparza." A blessing.

At intermission I couldn't settle, and so wandered around backstage, and found a kind of classroom behind the backstage area. And there was Stephen Sondheim, sitting at a desk by himself facing a chalkboard. He was wearing his tweedy brown jacket on this black-tie evening that patrons had paid hundreds of dollars to see. I put my hand on his back and asked if he was all right. I'd startled him, but he told me he was fine. Then he paused and looked up at me and said, "You made me cry." My god. I could hardly believe what he'd said to me. It took my breath away. I was deeply moved. I could only thank him quietly. Then I left him alone.

The Old Lady sings how things change, how things keep changing, and she implores her son to "quick, draw it all" before it disappears. I am now four years older than Stephen Sondheim was that summer, and I understand why that lyric might've moved him, why he might have been as moved as I am now when I see the world around me dissolving into something that has little resemblance to the world I knew as a younger woman. The Old Lady also sings "I see towers where there were trees." And we'd lost our towers the Fall just before. I couldn't sing that lyric without seeing those towers in my mind's eye. Maybe that had something to do with Sondheim's feelings as well. Maybe not. But things had certainly changed in our world in more ways than we might've yet understood. The Old Lady longs for the time "when things were truly beautiful." I believe that all of us who lived inside of Sondheim's music that summer were living in a place outside of time where things were beautiful. We were, as Stephen Holden titled his *New York Times* article, "Taking refuge in Sondheim's rare civility." The summer of 2002, we were all blessed.

On November twenty-sixth, 2021 nearly twenty years after that summer of rare civility, at age ninety-one, Stephen Sondheim passed away. And with his passing, I had the realization that my acting life has been measured by playing Sondheim roles. The ingenues, Philia in A FUNNY THING HAPPENED ON THE WAY TO THE FORUM, and Maria in WEST SIDE STORY. The young wife Amy in COMPANY. The middle-aged Desirée in A LITTLE NIGHT MUSIC, and The Stepmother in INTO THE WOODS. The older Heidi in FOLLIES. Finally, The Old Lady in SUNDAY IN THE PARK WITH GEORGE. My personal "ages of woman" expressed through the words and music of Stephen Sondheim. The master. I so miss him in the world.

arena stage

"The ferris wheel goes up, and then starts down."

Martha Hoch, BOOK OF DAYS

With the close of FRAME 312 at The Alliance in November, I was back in New York again going about the business of working to find the next work. It was holiday time, so Mama came up for Christmas and we again went to Town Hall to see *Prairie Home Companion* with Garrison Keillor, before it morphed into *Live From Here* with Chris Thiele. We revisited Radio City Music Hall for the Rockettes' Christmas show. We posed in front of the big red Christmas balls diagonally across the street from Radio City. A passer-by took our picture. It's a happy picture. I don't remember being quite as happy as the photo shows, but then I'm an actress, and so was she. We had done this Christmas ritual a few times now.

But it wasn't Christmas at home. New York didn't feel like my home any longer. It had become the place to get work. And now that I wasn't working in the city, the holiday was a little less exciting. Still, it was good to be able to give Mama a New York Christmas. That was at the heart of my personal celebration. It would be the last New York Christmas I'd give her.

Winter in New York was gray and the routine was growing tedious. The routine of setting up coffee with friends, seeing whatever show I could afford, going on auditions for plays mostly out of the city, hoping for work I would enjoy. Had I grown tired of the work? Maybe I was just tired. But yes, one of the auditions got me my next job—at Arena Stage in Washington, DC.

This was a Lanford Wilson play called BOOK OF DAYS which felt like home territory somehow. The Missouri writer's language was familiar to me, natural to deliver. The character I was cast as was not as familiar. She was the Dean of a Christian college, who'd never quite outgrown her Woodstock days. She was the hippie I never was but maybe should've been. I somehow missed the Sixties when I was in high school and college. I must've been too busy winning music contests and trying to get straight As. But I loved playing Martha Hoch. She was no-nonsense, strong, wise, had the language of a sailor, and was still young at age 60. I was again playing older than my real age, but not by much at that point. My actual age was catching up with my roles.

This was a great job, a wonderful ensemble of actors, a worthy play. But the world was still on alert since 9/11, and we were performing in the heart of our nation's capital. There were helicopters circling the city day and night, on watch for suspicious activity. They were a constant reminder of the insecurity of our world. It affected me deeply. I remember a nightmare when as I lay in bed in my actor housing, I looked up at the sky above me. There seemed to be no ceiling to the apartment, no roof. I lay there in the dream and watched as a bomb was falling from the sky directly toward me. It stopped maybe twenty feet above me and hovered. I was frozen, terrified. I woke suddenly, heart pounding, to the sound of a military helicopter passing over.

The run of BOOK OF DAYS at Arena was successful. Then, of course, it was back to New York and the same routine. My summer was free. No work presented itself. But there was a book or two to record. I had become Recorded Books' female voice of choice for Southern Christian romance. I suppose it was because I'd been the voice for *Gone with The Wind*. Also, I must carry Arkansas in my bones, my rhythms, my voice, even though I haven't lived there since I was four years old. I was grateful for the work. Thank God for Recorded Books. The work afforded me not only a fee for each book I'd record based on the book's finished length, but because it's union work through AFTRA, American Federation of TV and radio artists, it gave me insurance. So, when I hadn't worked the twenty weeks it took to qualify for insurance through Actor's Equity, AFTRA insurance would kick in. As insecure as the actor's profession is, our union insurance policies are strong. My three performer's unions, Equity, AFTRA and SAG—Screen Actors Guild—have excellent insurance plans. You have to work enough to qualify, but I somehow always did.

After three months offstage, another job came along, again through Susan Booth, Artistic Director of the Alliance Theatre. This was a shared production of a ten-actor, two-piano adaptation of MY FAIR LADY, number three for me. This time I was asked to play both Mrs. Higgins and Mrs. Pearce, Higgins' housekeeper. All the actors except for Henry and Eliza, played multiple roles. It was a clever idea, and also made producing this classic musical much more affordable for theatres.

However, this adaptation created by Gary Griffin was not built for one actress to play both older characters. Susan had rearranged the role designations. And it makes artistic sense for one actress to play both "mother" roles to Henry Higgins. But it made my job much harder than the audience would ever see. My backstage life was more complicated than it would have been if roles had been as assigned in Gary's adaptation. My show track was more difficult physically than it should have been.

The production was a long contract. It was a shared production among four theatres. It couldn't quite be called a tour, but it nearly was. We played the show for six months with enough time between cities to travel and remount the show in a new space. The production opened in October of 2003 at the St. Louis Rep. We performed the play in November/December at The Cincinnati Playhouse in the Park. January through March we played at Susan's theatre, and of course my home theatre in the early eighties, The Alliance in Atlanta. And finally, we played a theatre that originally wasn't part of the share, The Maltz-Jupiter Theatre in Jupiter, Florida. The Maltz-Jupiter was just reopening its doors, so I believe we were the first production in the newly refurbished theatre. Then we closed this shared production in April of 2004.

Florida in the spring was a welcome place to finish these six months of what was for me very hard work. I was tired. I took a week to rest and recover after we closed. Running the show had done me in. And this was new for me. I wasn't bouncing back so quickly as I was used to. I'd done a lot of emotional eating on the tour and was heavier now which was part of the problem. I had played the show well. I'd been praised for it in the reviews. But I'd had no personal need to play these characters, so rather than filling me up, the performing had drained me.

I'd never had trouble physically running a show, but with this run I was in pain daily. Back in New York I made an appointment with a

Brooklyn internist not far from where I lived. He diagnosed several low back herniated disks. He prescribed physical therapy, which was the first round of what would be years of PT to come. This had been a six-month job doing what felt like double duty. I was exhausted. Since my move to Caton Avenue in 2000, I'd had one job in New York, and nine jobs out-of-town, which meant nine temporary moves. Of course, I was exhausted.

Now I needed not only time to rest and heal, but space away from New York to look at my life, to reevaluate, to find what was important to me now. So, I found a subletter for four months, and did something I'd never done in my life. At age fifty-seven, I asked my mother if I could come live with her.

* * *

Mama was living in Ohio now, near my sister and brother-in-law. She'd taken a pretty serious fall when she was eighty, and because of the world's insecurity since 9/11, she'd felt the need to be living near family. I was still in New York working more out of town than intown, so Mama asked Lorna if she could come to Ohio to look for condos. How could Lorna say no? In 2002 in her early eighties, Mama had moved from Atlanta to Stow, Ohio.

When Mama was in her late eighties, she began to have some cognitive issues, and so she was moved into assisted living. Then in her mid-nineties, she was moved to memory care. In her late nineties, she began to struggle with repeated mini-strokes, but always she would rally. She was remarkable in that way. After each episode she'd be a little more compromised, but she refused to let go of her walker even though she really needed a wheelchair, until finally one episode took her ability to walk. From then, she had to be moved from bed to wheelchair to big chair and back again several times a day. Then three weeks after her last birthday she had another episode and a week after that she stopped eating. Two days later she finally let go her struggle less than a month after her ninety-eighth birthday. I wasn't with her on that Thanksgiving night, the night she passed, nor was my sister. But Lorna was a soldier through Mom's demise for the eight years she was in long-term care. Lorna was always there, always coming up with things to do to make Mom's life better. It wasn't easy for Lorna. Their relationship had always been difficult. And so, it was ironic that Mama ended up depending on Lorna for her physical needs in her later life. But maybe not so ironic. Maybe that's exactly the way it was supposed to be. And Lorna was always there. Lorna was always problem solving. Lorna was present. Lorna was a rock.

The weekend just after Mom's ninety-eighth birthday on Halloween, 2019, I'd driven to visit my family. Mama and I had a sweet goodbye. She'd been moved from her wheelchair to a big chair in the group living room and was watching a film with a few other residents. LES MISERABLES was the film they were watching which seemed oddly appropriate. I sat with her and watched the film for a while. She asked me if I needed anything. A better chair? Did I need a cup of coffee? She was playing the role of hostess she had always played. She wasn't my beautiful Mama anymore. Age and illness had thinned her hair and ravaged her skin. If she could've seen herself, she would've been embarrassed. But there is some grace in dementia, cruel disease that it is, because she was not fully aware of what her life had become. When I left her sitting there, I told her that I loved her, and she said to me, "Oh, I love you too, Sweetie!" with the biggest smile on her face. And as I backed away waving, she looked like a little girl waving back to me, still wearing that big smile. That was a gift. Three weeks from then, she would be gone.

Up until the end, Mama was doing what she'd always done, she was surviving. She's who taught me to survive. And I miss her. I miss her all dressed up, hair and makeup done to perfection. I miss her talking about what I did that made her proud whether she understood it or not. I miss her coming to New York to visit at Christmastime, when we'd go to Radio City Music Hall to see the Rockettes, then watch the skaters at Rockefeller Center underneath the big Christmas tree. I miss her traveling to see me in plays all over the country. I miss her being proud of me. I miss her telling me "It was a good show."

CHAPTER TWENTY

blessings

"There is magic in the ground under the city"

In 2004, two years after my mother had moved to Ohio, I was asking to come live with her while I figured out my life. And when I first asked, she said no. Oh, my goodness, I wasn't expecting that. It didn't make me angry so much as surprised, and a little embarrassed. Mama had never told me how she felt when I moved back to New York from Atlanta, and left her without family nearby. Now I wondered how she'd really felt. Mama could be secretive. If she needed me to stay in Atlanta, I wish she'd told me. She was a fiercely independent woman, so without her asking me to stay, I'd assumed she understood and was OK with my leaving. I thought she had given me her blessing.

I wondered, was she telling me now that I'd hurt her by leaving? Was she punishing me by not allowing me to come "home" now? No, she wasn't. What she had actually said was that her condo was very small, and she wasn't sure there'd be enough room for the two of us, her cat, and my two cats. I'd immediately backed down and told her to forget I'd asked, not to give it another thought.

But the next day she called and told me that of course I should come. I thanked her, and I did come. I schlepped Charlie and Daisy in Mama's Oldsmobile from Brooklyn to her condo in Stow, Ohio. And for four months I lived with my mother. We made it work somehow. We went to afternoon movies. We took day trips. We spent time with Lorna and Mark. I joined a gym and worked out daily. It was a kind of vacation for me, but one with a looming decision to make. I needed to figure out what to do next with my life.

Should I leave showbiz entirely and move to Ohio where my family was? If I did, what would I do there? I couldn't afford to stop working yet. I'd have to travel to Cleveland for the closest professional regional theatre and then if I was lucky enough to be cast at Cleveland Playhouse, it would be for only one show, possibly two shows in a season. Did I go back to New York and do a major push for work in the city? Get new headshots, lose weight, re-introduce myself to the casting people? But at my age would that be too little too late? Or did I move back to Chicago as I should have done instead of moving to Atlanta? That seemed the smartest move, one that could promise ongoing work in one town, and in a town where I had an established reputation.

I decided to make a trip to Chicago to talk with people and explore the possibility. I called my friend Rick Boynton, now the Creative Producer at Chicago Shakespeare, but who was then artistic director of The Marriott Lincolnshire Theatre. He and I had acted together at The Marriott in that lovely production of Schmidt/Jones' GROVERS CORNERS in the late eighties. Rick generously offered to put me up in The Lincolnshire Resort while I looked at apartments and talked with casting people in Chicago. So, I made the six-hour drive and settled in for a time to re-imagine a life in Chicago.

I spent a lot of time alone in the room at the Marriott, questioning myself, looking at the last dozen years of my life from Chicago to New York to Atlanta to New York again. I asked myself if I was just plowing up old ground contemplating another move. I observed myself, how tired I was. "World-weary" is not too strong to describe how I felt. I asked myself what was I doing? I honestly didn't know. I didn't know anything but that something had to change. I couldn't continue walking the treadmill I'd been on the last three years without ending up in the hospital or worse.

What did I want? What was I looking for? Was it finally, simply, home? Atlanta had been my only true home as an adult. But going back had shown me that not only had time gone by, but the place itself had passed away. I realized that the reason you can't go back is not simply because times have changed, but because the home you're trying to go back to has physically disappeared.

Would I have the same experience in Chicago if I were to move back? But Chicago had never really been home so much as a place of transition. I wouldn't be moving back to find home again. I'd be moving to find work. And maybe this time Chicago might become my home. It made practical sense. But I was struggling emotionally with something I couldn't define. I was deeply confused, going over what might be best for me, what I wanted, what I should do. I felt completely alone. The only thing I could do, the only thing I wanted to do was cry. So, I allowed myself to do so, sitting in that hotel room for days, until there were no more tears.

Then one morning I woke clear-headed, thinking about Milwaukee, how its name in Potawatomi—*minwaking*—means "the gathering place by the waters." I was compelled to drive the hour-and-a-half North to that gathering place, and found my way to a bench in Klode Park, high on a bluff overlooking Lake Michigan.

I sat and watched as the sunset glowing orange behind me turned the sky over the Great Lake in front of me a deep lavender, and it was breathtaking. It moved me to remember that as an out-of-towner working at The Rep how much I had loved the pastel winter skies over the Wisconsin countryside. I knew in my heart that I needed to live in a place filled with natural beauty, and that this might be the place. The sunset over Lake Michigan was inviting me. What I would do, where I would live, I didn't know. But sitting on a bluff by the Great Lake, it came clear that for now, Milwaukee was the place I wanted, maybe even needed to be.

I drove back to the Marriott and gave my deep thanks to Rick, because without his generosity I wouldn't have had the time and space away from New York, away from my family, away from the comfort of my animals, to go through a kind of dark night of the soul, and wake up with clarity. I drove back to Mama's home to share my decision. It made sense to her too. I left my cats with her, drove back to New York to arrange for a moving company, let go my lease, and flew to Milwaukee to find an apartment which presented itself within a few days. It was the lower level of a 1920's duplex in Shorewood, a village adjoining the city of Milwaukee. The apartment was in the process of being refurbished. I walked through the open front door of the house and asked a workman who to speak to about renting the place. He called the landlady, and then and there we made a deal over the phone that for $750 a month's rent plus deposit, I could live in this wonderful old two-bedroom flat with windows all around, a porch and a garden ... a garden! I hadn't had a garden for twenty years. Wonderful!

So, I flew back to New York to finish packing and wait for the moving truck. Then I drove to Ohio and spent a couple of nights with my family. Finally, the kitties and I drove the eight hours to Milwaukee, a drive I would make many times in the coming years. We three slept in a Milwaukee motel for a night. Then on January fifth, the Twelfth Day of Christmas 2005, Charlie and Daisy and I moved into this lovely old house in this lovely old tree-lined neighborhood, not twelve blocks from Great Lake Michigan. And I felt like I could breathe again.

When I told my friends I was moving from New York to Milwaukee, the first question from nearly everybody was "Why Milwaukee?" I couldn't explain. My first answer was theatre. I had twenty years professional history with The Rep. Milwaukee has six Equity Houses including The Rep, and a slew of smaller theatres established for years with followings of their own. Milwaukee is a town that loves and supports all its arts. I knew I could continue to work in the city. But my move to Milwaukee meant more to me than working in the theatre.

In the early eighties, I'd taken myself on an audition tour. I'd driven from Atlanta, north through the Midwest auditioning at several theatres along the way, and the final two theatres on my tour were The Goodman in Chicago and The Milwaukee Rep. I'll never forget driving into Milwaukee from the South on I-94, seeing this "city of spires" on the horizon. I had a visceral response. I felt I knew the place.

John Dillon was Artistic Director of The Rep then. And though he certainly knew my work from the past, I wanted to re-introduce myself and let him know I was now available for out-of-town work. Larry was alive then and a company member at the Rep. Thanks to John, Larry was in the process of writing the plays that would eventually make him famous. We shared some happy times together that trip. Lots of laughter. It was impossible to be with Larry and not laugh. We were pals. I couldn't know then that it would be the last time I'd see Larry. There in his room at The Plaza Motor Hotel with the wall-high wooden bookshelves that we'd built together when we were company members at The Harlequin DC in the seventies. We'd broken those shelves down and brought them with us when The Harlequin moved to Atlanta. Then he'd broken them down again and brought them with him to Milwaukee after our divorce. There they were, a piece of our lives together living with him in Milwaukee.

Years later, I realized that every one of my family had come to visit me in Milwaukee when I myself had been working out-of-town, living with my dear Katydid Kirkland McDougal at The Plaza Motor Hotel. Larry's dear parents Dolores and Percy, his remarkable sister Jackie, my sweet Daddy and independent Mama, my second husband Kent who'd directed two shows at The Rep. Even my Harlequin family, Jack and Michele Kyirieleison had stayed at The Plaza while Jack was working at The Rep. All my family had been in Milwaukee before I ever moved to the city. All except my sister. Then fourteen years after I made the move, Lorna came with her mensch of a husband Mark. Now everyone I call family, everyone I love had left their energy, their love with me in Milwaukee. I'd acquired a hometown through my work.

In 1990 when I'd been doing DRIVING MISS DAISY as an out-of-towner at The Rep, one night during tech rehearsals I had a dream about our props guy Jeff, an earthy fella, with his gnarled hands and long white wispy hair and beard. In the dream he came to me and shook a small cloth pouch near my face and spoke some words that I can't quite call up. The next day before rehearsal I told Jeff about the dream and he said to me, "Well, ya know, yesterday I blessed the power place backstage with my pouch." It's a ritual he did every show with his pouch filled with gatherings—stones, feathers, pieces of wood and whatever else presented itself as worthy to be held in his bag of talismans. The "power place" he blessed had been the center of the power plant that occupied the building before The Rep was built inside the bones of the plant. And many years before the place was occupied by a power plant, it was occupied by a different kind of power. Long before the city was even thought of, the space where The Rep stands had been the ritual gathering place of Native American Tribes living by the river. The Milwaukee Rep sits next to the Milwaukee River on a place of long-held power. A gathering place by the waters. Jeff told me he claimed to know the central point of power in the ground under the theatre. It's the place where he did his ritual blessing before the mounting of each new production, backstage a little right of center. So, before every performance of DAISY, I would go backstage a little right of center, walk in a circle around what I believed must surely be the place of power and offer a blessing of my own. A blessing of thanks. Because there is magic in the ground under the city.

milwaukee

"Lately, I been addin' things up."

Betty Meeks, THE FOREIGNER

The last play I did at The Milwaukee Rep was THE FOREIGNER by Larry Shue. It was the fourth production to be mounted by The Rep, which had premiered the play in 1983. The Rep announced it as their Christmas show for the 2016/17 season. And since I'd never read the play, I'm only a little embarrassed to admit, it was long-past time I did. I got a copy from the library and half-way through my read, I realized that one of the ways Larry had worked through our divorce, was to put me in the play as the absent wife of the lead character, Charlie. We believe she's dying of a terminal illness but in the end, she recovers fully and runs off with a proctologist. Of course. It's classic Larry. And as it should be, the joke is on me.

Reading the play, I couldn't help but remember Mama Shue who'd come back into my life when I showed up at Larry's funeral. I'd missed her. She'd been a girlfriend like my mother. I knew Larry had not based the character of Betty Meeks on Mama Shue, but a few friends who knew Larry's mother and had seen other productions, thought that Betty was in fact based on Dolores Shue. She may not have been the old country woman in Larry's story, but I felt that Betty Meeks carried Mama Shue's heart. I began to wonder if I could play Betty Meeks. I wasn't exactly right for her, but I loved her down-home funny-wise spirit. And I felt I understood her. So, when I got a call that very day from JC Clementz, casting director at the Rep saying that the director, Laura Gordon wanted to know if I'd like to play the role of Betty Meeks, I was somehow not surprised. I told him I was having a hip replacement on the Ides of March. He said the play didn't go into rehearsal till nearly the Ides of October, and I'd surely be fine by then. Laura Gordon is a superb actress and a fine director. I'd worked with her twice before, and she's one of the directors I've enjoyed working with most. So, since Laura had asked, I told JC I'd be happy to play Betty Meeks.

Jim Pickering is the premiere actor of the Milwaukee Rep. He's been a company member longer than any other actor in the city. He'd be playing Froggy opposite my Betty in our production. Jim had played the title role in the original production of Larry's THE NERD. He'd also played Charlie in The Rep's second production of THE FOREIGNER in 1992. Jim and Larry had been Rep company members together in the seventies, and no one understands Larry's comedy better than Jim does.

Jim and I had acted together more than a few times since 1985 when I'd first been called to The Rep. So, working with Jim again especially in a Larry Shue play was wonderful, like coming home. On a particularly long tech rehearsal day while we were sitting around backstage waiting to be called, Jim shared a bit of Pickering wisdom with me. "There are two kinds of people in the world. Those who do eight shows a week, and those who don't." He was being only slightly facetious. But still, during the run of our show, much as I loved playing Larry's wickedly smart comedy, I was reminded how hard it is to do eight shows a week. And as our run progressed, I began to think I might be ready to be one of "those who don't."

I like to call THE FOREIGNER my swan song, though I've done one play since for Renaissance Theatreworks. It's a popular play called NATIVE GARDENS. I played my character responsibly as I always do, but I didn't like her much. And I'd taken the role for the wrong reasons. It was offered, and I didn't know what else to do. I learn my life lessons slowly. When you've been an actor for as long as I have, it's hard to simply stop. When performing has defined so much of who you are, it's hard to walk away. But I've come to realize in my bones, literally, that while acting will forever be my work, it is no longer my life.

It's seventeen years since my move to Milwaukee. I'm no longer living in the tree-lined neighborhood of Shorewood, no longer living with Buddha Cat Charlie and sweet Daisy cat. They've both crossed over the Rainbow Bridge. Now I'm living in the village of Fox Point in an apartment with a balcony overlooking a pond, sharing my country-in-the-city home with another beautiful boy cat named Robin Goodfellow, black of coat, green of eye, loud of mouth, and at sixteen years old, a dear, dear companion to me.

Milwaukee has given me work and the city has given me friends, more than a few of whom have become like family. Still up until recently, I've been reluctant to call Milwaukee home. It's as though I've been rushing through life on a kind of kinetic energy, the energy generated from my seventy-five years of moving from city to city. I've never fully committed to any community because I've always been in motion until Atlanta for a number of years, and now Milwaukee for these seventeen. But even here I've been in motion. And my first years here, I wasn't sure I'd stay. I was experiencing in Milwaukee something of what I'd felt in Atlanta when I'd moved back from New York. I felt my accomplishments in New York and Chicago weren't fully appreciated.

I understand now that some of what I felt was born out of my own need to belong to a community. When I moved to here, if I belonged to the community in any way, it was as an extended company member of The Rep years before, when John Dillon was Artistic Director. I suppose I expected to be folded into the Rep's company once I moved to the city. But like times change, and cities change, companies change. The Rep's company was not the one I had worked with in the late eighties. And now there was no real place for me, because actresses change too, and now I was older. The current Rep company had no need for an older actress. The truth is that no resident company has need of more than one of us who has reached an age when we've become "one of them," as my first agent had once so rudely labeled us. If we haven't found our way into a resident company by age forty-five or fifty, it's most likely too late. The Rep had Jim Pickering's wife, Rose who'd been first blessed at The Rep for at least thirty years. The brilliant American Players Theatre in Spring Green, WI, has only one older actress in its core company, Sarah Day, who's been with her company for years. And I remember in the Rep's exchange with The Omsk State Drama Theatre, that there was only one older actress in their Russian company. Truth. It was a hard truth to face because I so longed to be part of a company again. The Harlequin had trained me to be a company actor in my twenties. Working with so many of the same actors at The Alliance in my thirties was like working within a company. Even playing on Broadway for a year and a half in my forties felt like being part of a resident company. Then after DAMN YANKEES closed, throughout my fifties, my work was entirely freelance.

I didn't move to Milwaukee till I was nearly sixty. Now fifteen years later, The Rep's resident company is no longer. A few years after my move, the resident company was rearranged and company members were given a different label, "associate artists." But with that new name, though the actors were still considered for roles, they were no longer promised work. And with the loss of that guarantee went the promise of ongoing insurance. The acting company has been dispersed. And that's a huge loss for Milwaukee.

To be fair, most of the large regional theatres in the country operate on this same paradigm. It took The Rep a few years longer to decide to join the movement away from theatre centered around its actors. And I like to think that the reason it took longer in Milwaukee is that the Rep audience loved its actors. The acting company belonged to their audience.

I'm happy I got to play with that company now and again over twenty-five years. But I'm sorry I never got to belong to The Rep audience. When you live and work in one place all your life, the audience sees the young characters you played inside your older ones. They see your Eliza and Guinevere inside every Fraulein Schneider and Florence Foster Jenkins you play. No one here saw my Gertrude or Desirée or Mrs. Anna. So, I've sometimes felt like Sir Andrew Aguecheek in Shakespeare's TWELFTH NIGHT who says, "I was adored once too." We audiences all "adore" our younger characters. We are all drawn to our coming-of-age stories. It seems to be human nature. I know I'm respected by the Milwaukee theatre community. I just I wish I hadn't arrived too late to play my Blanche DuBois for them.

I am grateful to the Milwaukee theatre community for putting me to work so quickly after my move, because I couldn't afford to stop working quite yet. I'm grateful to all the union theatres in town for hiring me—The Milwaukee Rep, Milwaukee Chamber Theatre, Renaissance Theatreworks, Next Act Theatre, Skylight Music Theatre and First Stage Children's Theatre. They have all given me wonderful roles to play. I thank all my Milwaukee directors, Monty Davis first, who has now passed on, but who'd offered me a role in BRIGHTON BEACH MEMOIRS at his Chamber Theatre, months before I actually made the move. His offer was an affirmation that my decision to come was good. And for the roles I've been given in Milwaukee that I'm particularly happy to have played, thanks to Bill Theisen at Skylight for Florence Foster Jenkins in SOUVENIR, to Suzan Fete at Renaissance for Helen Martins in THE ROAD TO MECCA, to David Cecsarini at Next Act for Sonia in a new play by Richard Lyons Conlon called ONE TIME and for Minka in Jeffrey Hatcher's MURDERERS, to Laura Gordon for Maggie in MEMORY HOUSE at Renaissance, and at The Rep for Nancy in SEASCAPE as well as Betty Meeks in THE FOREIGNER, to Joseph Hanreddy, former Artistic Director of The Milwaukee Rep, for Hattie Sederholm in TEN CHIMNEYS, and to Mark Clements, current Artistic Director of The Rep, for Fraulein Schneider in CABARET.

Since the move, I've done thirteen plays in Milwaukee, and seven plays out of town in Atlanta, Tucson, Phoenix, Knoxville, and Chicago. I've recorded ten books and created four cabarets, with three extraordinary pianists—Jack Forbes Wilson, Jamie Johns, and David Bonofiglio. Peppered through all that performing, I've had four joint replacements—two knees, and two hips. Fifty years is a long time to put the body through the rigors of stage acting. But finally, thanks to the work and my unions, I've become an old-age pensioner.

Nearly all my life I've tried to leave the theatre. I suppose it started in my early forties when it seemed as if the theatre was leaving me, when I felt I was being seen for roles too old for me. I'm not alone in that feeling. But I think my pull to leave the theatre is about more than aging. I have often felt on some deep level that I was doing the wrong work, that I should have been a musician or a teacher or a classical chamber singer. And I could have been any one of those, if the pull to follow those calls was stronger. But after years of soul-searching, I've come to accept that my strongest call was to be an actor.

Now fifty years since I played my first role, auditions are still being offered, though the roles are less interesting to me. I've had so many beautiful characters to play, so many brilliant writers to interpret, that just standing on a stage is not enough. The role has to have some meaning for me before I am able to give myself to it fully. Acting is hard work. I don't perform for attention only. Most of the time, I'd still rather hide. I perform for the joy of feeling the words and music move through me and out into the audience, to share the experience that we all create together. For the last twenty years I've thought the next role would be my last, almost wished it would be my last, while at the same time hoping for another that might demand the best of me. It's been three years since I stood in front of a theatre audience. Is the push and tug finally over? I wonder, am I finally finished?

It's a moot point now as I've written through the long winters of 2020/21 and into the winter of 2022. The decision seems to have been made for me. And I wonder if when this pandemic has completely passed, will theatre exist as it did in "the before time." Most theatres now offer virtual productions, alongside in-person performances. But well-done as many of these offerings are, theatre filmed live is not, cannot be the same as watching actors on the stage in the moment. The audience changes the energy in the room. The audience is partner in the storytelling. Still, theatres are becoming better at putting plays on film, and we in the audience are becoming accustomed to watching theatre on film. I wonder if when the threat of the pandemic has passed completely, will we still love sitting in the theatre as much as we did before? We do seem to be changing, in ways that are hard to fully understand.

Maybe we've been given this time away from "normal life" to look at ourselves. As we've been asked to distance from one another, we've been given the opportunity to look at how the society we've built has created more and more distance between those who have and those who have not. As the demonstrations began in response to the police murder of George Floyd in Minneapolis, our society has begun to awaken to the reality of inherent white privilege, maybe not for the first time, but more clearly, more deeply now.

I've been shown my own white privilege. Hard as my acting life has been, I would not have been given this life in the theatre if I had been African American, Hispanic, Asian or Native American. The roles I've played simply would not have been available to me, and even if they were, I would most likely have lost them to white actresses. Truth. I know that now. I know that because our society is shifting. We are finally opening our eyes to the racism that our privilege has been built on, and we can never go back. Now I see that I have lived and continue to live a privileged life.

So, I write this memoir about my privileged life in the theatre, because I am shifting, and I cannot believe I've been given a life in the theatre. And how lucky I am that for the last two years, since the theatre was on hold because the rest of the world was on hold, I no longer had to work to make ends meet because of pensions from the work I already did through my life in the theatre. For fifty years. And it has been a privilege. All my life I have been blessed.

What I could not have known in writing this memoir, is how the themes running through my personal life would come so clear in remembering my life in the theatre. Naivete, survival, struggle with age, struggle with drink, search for home, partnering animals, magical thinking, and constant seeking. I could not have realized without looking at my life in the theatre how bonded I've remained with my family. All of them now gone. Except for sisters.

Larry's sister Jackie, my sister-in-law by ex-marriage has somehow stayed in my life through all our passages for fifty-two years. But the most important person in my life is my only sister, Lorna. Until a few years ago Lorna and I were not close. I left my parents' home at age seventeen, and my sister was only ten. So as adults, we have been playing catchup. And as many people told us, we would grow closer through the long eight years of our mother's demise. Lorna and I have been learning one another. And now that I know her better, the truest things I know are that she is sentimental like I am, hard-headed like I am, honest like I am, more grounded than I am, and has a heart of gold that's way bigger than mine. I miss her. Maybe, with the spring I can travel to see her and Mark again. That would be the best of blessings.

So, what now? In the past when I thought I was finished acting, when there'd been nothing on the horizon for months, always at the eleventh hour some work would show itself. And often the role would resonate my life's passage at the time. There was a kind of magic in the way these characters presented themselves just when I was ready to hear what they had to say.

Lizzie Curry in 110 IN THE SHADE taught me to honor my simple little dreams. Emily Stilson in WINGS taught me to see life as an adventure. Hannah Jelkes in THE NIGHT OF THE IGUANA taught me to accept whatever situation presents itself. Helen Martins in THE ROAD TO MECCA taught me to be led by the artist in me. Betty Meeks in THE FOREIGNER taught me to remember always the joy of living. Courageous characters, all. They uncover the best in me.

I thought I was writing my story for aspiring young actors, so they might consider the reality of a working actor's life. I thought I was writing my story for "civilians" so they might understand that not every successful actor reaches movie-star fame. But now, I believe I've written my story so I might forgive myself for years of struggle with a profession that often took more than it gave. But alongside the struggle, I have felt a sense of purpose. And through it all, I have loved the work. So, I have to believe that the work I did is the work I was supposed to do.

I wonder. When the theatre calls again, will I find myself drawn back to the stage? I honestly don't know. I do know my desire to exercise "that sacred communion between actor and audience" will never die. And maybe, born out of my history in the theatre, from the characters that I've played and the cities where I've lived, a different way of exercising "that sacred communion" will appear. Maybe a new kind of work will show itself. Or maybe I'll finally learn to be fully present to whatever appears. Grateful to be here, in this gathering place by the waters, that for now, I call home.

THE END